Daily Meditations (with Scripture) for Busy Grandmas

Revised Edition

Theresa Cotter

ACTA

ASSISTING CHRISTIANS TO ACT

PUBLICATIONS

Daily Meditations (with Scripture) for Busy Grandmas
Revised Edition
by Theresa Cotter

Edited by Gregory F. Augustine Pierce
Cover design by Tom A. Wright
Design and Typesetting by Desktop Edit Shop, Inc.

Published by   ACTA Publications
                Assisting Christians to Act
                4848 N. Clark Street
                Chicago, Illinois 60640
                312-271-1030

Library of Congress Catalog number: 96-85734

ISBN: 0-87946-148-9

Printed in the United States of America
Year: 09 08 07 06 05 04 03
Printing: 10 9 8 7 6 5 4 3 2 1

Contents

Dedication

*Once again, to Jack,
for all the obvious reasons…
and more.*

Introduction to the Revised Edition

What would you like to change?" the editor asked, after informing me that the "Grandma" book would be reissued. "Any corrections or additions?"

Well having been blessed with more grandchildren and more years of living, of course I have more to say!

If I were writing this book today I would stress the educational opportunities for us older students through colleges and universities, churches, synagogues and mosques, and, of course, the enriching Elderhostel program. We seniors make the best students, for we learn for the sheer joy and love of learning!

If I could, I would promote more prayer and, inspired by the Spirit, more activism. We grandmas can write letters and emails, make presentations and phone calls, march in demonstrations. The world needs our wisdom and experience!

If I could, I would super-emphasize the awareness of this moment. To stress the importance of *living today fully* I would *italicize* extensively and end those sentences with an overabundance of exclamation points!!!

If I could rewrite this book—in any way—I would encourage a deeper faith in God and self and others, especially our children and grandchildren. I would write in huge, inspiring, three-dimensional letters, letters large enough to support us, and strong enough to cling to in times of waning faith.

If I could, I would write a book that played music when opened: classical and inspirational music, sentimental love songs, pop tunes and lullabies, nurturing melodies from around the world, bird songs and baby-coos and whispers of "I love you."

If I could, I would sprinkle joy throughout the pages, cartoons and jokes accompanied with giggles, titters, laughter.

If I could, I would endow these words-on-paper with the scents of spring flowers, line-dried laundry, fresh bread, real Christmas trees, campfires and newly-mowed grass.

If I could, I would include art work and photos: landscapes so vivid we could travel the roads; classics that remind us of our roots; impressionist works to affect our hearts; modern art to awaken our lazy imaginations; beauty to touch our souls.

If I could, I would enhance this volume with the feel of a freshly-made bed, a cool summer breeze, the sensation of loved ones held close, the touch of satin and baby-skin, that comfortable fullness after a favorite meal, the pleasure of being affirmed, the experience of being divinely loved.

If I could, I would embody this volume with tranquility and compassion, respect and understanding, love and well-being, serenity and joy.

And somewhere in this book, dear reader, you would be assured that you are treasured by this writer.

January 1   My Favorite Year

This is my favorite year!

This year, this month, this day, this very minute—each is my favorite. It is here that I exist; it is now that I live.

I accept this new year which begins today. I readily open my hands to receive this wonderful gift of time from God.

I accept its happiness gladly.

I accept its sorrows, knowing that I shall learn compassion from them.

I accept its losses, making room in my life for what is new.

I accept its doubts and questions and uncertainties, which send me searching for God.

In faith and with joy I affirm: This is my favorite year!

Arise, shine; for your light has come, and the glory of the LORD has risen upon you.

Isaiah 60:1

January 2   ABCs

Surely we've read our quota of *ABC* books: A is for *apple* (or *auto*, or *aardvark*, or *Alpha Centauri*, or *anything*!)

Using these ABCs and Mother Goose and Dr. Seuss, the Aesop fables and Bible stories and Sesame Street books, we've amused, distracted, taught, nurtured, inspired our kids and now our grandkids.

And we've read to them because we love doing it.

But those rhymes and stories are also ways of putting order to the world, of explaining our culture and our religious beliefs, of growing in our understanding of the life that we—children and parents and grandparents—are living.

In these readings we recall the past, treasure the present moment, and look forward in faith. With those stories we are affirming that there really is a rhyme/reason for it all.

For wisdom will come into your heart, and knowledge will be pleasant to your soul.

Proverbs 2:10

January 3   Benchmarkers

S ome kids, in the process of becoming adults, board an emotional roller-coaster. During these less-than-amusing times we adults need to remind ourselves that we are not responsible for reconstructing their series of hills and valleys into a straight and level freeway.

What young people need are stable benchmarks with which to gauge their ups and downs. They do not need adults who are unpredictable or who overreact to their every idiosyncrasy.

Parents, who are so intimately involved in their children's lives, may sometimes find it difficult to provide those benchmarks.

On the other hand, we grandmothers, because we've garnered a broader perspective on life—and because we've survived the development of our own kids—can provide that stability. We can be benchmarkers to our grandchildren.

Set up road markers for yourself, make yourself guideposts; consider well the highway, the road by which you went.

Jeremiah 31:21

Although the ink is faint on those yellowed, brittle pages, the familiar rhyme is still legible:

First comes love and then comes marriage;
Then comes Theresa with a baby carriage.

Way-back-when, that couplet described what most of us believed to be the predictable order of these significant events. Times have changed, however. That baby-in-the-carriage may have been adopted into a "significant relationship" or into sharing an adult's single life; that baby may only ever know one parent; that baby may have had laboratory assistance with conception or borrowed a uterus for its first home. Thus some of us become grandparents without ever becoming in-laws.

Adherence to convention means nothing to that newborn babe or the adopted youth. Our grandchild knows only the need to be loved, the need to be accepted, and the need to be grandparented.

That little girl, unaware of modes of propriety, still seeks acceptance. That young boy, heedless of society's condonation or condemnation, still needs guidance. That adolescent still needs roots and wings and stories and an abundance of grand-times!

Despite the circumstances of our grandchild's birth or life, our job as grandma remains unchanged.

> **From his fullness we have all received, grace**
> **upon grace.**

John 1:16

Eventually the realization arrives. It may come gradually or it may come like a bolt of lightning. No matter how it arrives, it is a powerful moment to realize that my baby, my young-

11

ster, my teenager is now an adult!

It is a shock to realize that the child who has been so dependent upon me for what seems like forever no longer needs me. It is a shock to realize that my offspring is no longer emotionally tied to me as in the past.

It is an additional shock to realize how tight the emotional ties are binding me to my adult-child.

Love never ends.

1 Corinthians 13:8

January 6   Beginnings

Beginnings are important.

If the beginning of a book is not appealing, the book will not be read.

If the beginning of a building is not strong and firm, the building will not last.

The beginnings of humanity, the beginnings of our religion, the beginnings of this country, the beginnings of each individual—all are significant.

The first clue to directions, destinations, endings is contained in beginnings.

In the beginning was the Word, and the Word was with God, and the Word was God.

John 1:1

January 7   Chicken Soup

Recently, scientists discovered a mysterious something in chicken soup that really does help sick people recover more rapidly.

Are we grandmas supposed to be surprised at the news? Every maternal-type since Eve has known that there is great curative power in chicken soup!

> *It will be a healing for your flesh*
> *and a refreshment for your body.*

Proverbs 3:8

January 8 — Double Standards

Discrimination!" "Injustice!" "Double standard!"
These terms are the ultimate cry of outrage by emerging teens and all who believe in the triumph of justice.

However, by the age of grandmotherhood we have learned that life often does present situations where we *should* impose a double standard. One child matures more rapidly than another; one child's needs are more critical than another's; times and situations are always changing; our own maturity and its accompanying insights produce different standards. And we do learn—from our correct decisions and from our mistakes.

Often it comes down to the basic realization that justice is best served when influenced by compassion, experience, knowledge, and love.

> *Now we have received not the spirit of the*
> *world, but the Spirit that is from God, so that*
> *we may understand the gifts bestowed on us by*
> *God.*

1 Corinthians 2:12

January 9   Failure

Failure is a word that can be used to describe an event, a plan, an attempt, a strategy, a recipe, an offense, an experiment, a venture, an enterprise, a project, an adventure, a gamble, an idea, a scheme, a device, an appliance, a method, an undertaking, a suggestion, a defense, a design, a procedure, an experience, a happening—but never, ever a person.

> *God's temple is holy, and you are that temple.*
>
> **1 Corinthians 3:17**

January 10   First Grandchild

For many, our lifelong dream is to touch immortality. We fear being forgotten—which is a large part of our fear of death. Thus we often spend our lives in fruitless efforts to leave our mark upon the world.

And then, in that tiny newborn life of our first grandchild, we recognize our own immortality.

> *There was also a prophet, Anna...of a great age....She came, and began to praise God and to speak about the child to all who were looking for the redemption of Jerusalem.*
>
> **Luke 2:36,38**

January 11   Fortune Cookies

Being fond of the food of various Asian cultures, I've consumed my share of fortune cookies. That means I've also received lots of *fortunes*.

Of these many cookie-wrapped fortunes, some were obviously more appropriate than others; some I simply dismissed; some were twenty years too late; some I did not understand; some brought laughter and others tears.

A few fortunes I carried home and placed on my bulletin board, where they continue to cheer me, remind me of my goals, or express a gem of a thought.

But life itself is like a bowl overflowing with fortune cookies containing messages from the media, from friends, from family, from books and magazines, from Scripture, from the God within us.

Of these variously delivered fortunes, some are obviously more appropriate than others; some we may dismiss; some are twenty years too late; some we do not understand; some bring laughter and others tears. And some are gems worth preserving.

We are free to choose the *fortunes* we make our own.

You are the light of the world.

Matthew 5:14

January 12   Listeners

I've learned that when one of my grandkids says, "Grandma, let's talk!" that usually means, "Grandma, please listen!" And listening is something that we grandmas usually do well.

We can listen with acceptance, wisdom and experience. We can also listen compassionately, lovingly and nonjudgmentally.

Such patient listening rewards us abundantly, for we become confidantes of the young and privileged sharers of their hopes and fears, pains and dreams.

Let everyone be quick to listen, slow to speak,
slow to anger.

James 1:19

January 13   God's Grandchildren

God has no grandchildren." That's what the young priest said in his homily.

But what does *he* know?

I realize he meant that each of us receives the full force of God's love and mercy, undiluted through intermediaries. But his statement also indicates that the young priest doesn't understand grandparenthood.

I know that the love of a grandmother for a grandchild is not lessened because of the intervening generation. Oh no! The unmeasurable love of a parent for a child is somehow increased, added to, magnified, expanded. That is the nature of a grandparent's love.

There is a Greek saying: The child of my child is twice my child.

> *You are precious in my sight, and honored, and*
> *I love you.*

Isaiah 43:4

January 14   Prayer of a Grandmother

God of Love,

You have chosen me to share with you in the continuing act of creation.

May I come to understand more deeply,

through my parenting,

how important I am to you, my Creator.

You have chosen me to join with you in the nurturing of the young.

May I experience more fully,

through my parenting,

your love for me, your child.

You have chosen me to taste of everlasting life through being a
     grandparent.
May there be ignited within me,
through my grandmothering,
wisdom and compassion toward all your children.

I ask these things in the name of Christ, who is brother to us all.
     Amen.

Woman, great is your faith!
Matthew 15:28

January 15   Hope

What is life—if we have not hope?
     Of course we need hope to protect us from despera-
tion and despair. But we also need hope to protect us
from those devious demons of lethargy and complacency.

It takes courage to go beyond the usual, comfortable confines of
our lives and risk floundering or embarrassment or criticism or
failure.

Consider a seed; only after the embryo plant leaves the security
of its seed-womb and thrusts forth its shoot into the unfamiliar environment of the world can it come to fruition. Without hope and
courage to take this risk it dies unfulfilled.

So it is with us grandmothers. Extending ourselves and taking
risks is a scenario we need to continue throughout life. The virtue
of hope is what gives us both the impetus and the direction for such
courageous action.

*For it is God who is at work in you, enabling
you both to will and to work for his good pleasure.*

Philippians 2:13

17

January 16   It's Fun!

Why is grandmothering so much fun?
Of the various answers to that question, one worth considering is that we grandmas have finally gotten past the "trying-to-be-perfect" stage.

By the time we've become grandmas we realize that we can only be who we are. We can only do our best.

How liberating is this realization. This self-acceptance also enables us to accept our grandchild as a unique person and a reflection of a different face of God.

So whether we teach our granddaughter tatting or karate, offer our grandson gourmet cooking recipes or business administration strategies, or just envelop them both with our love, it's okay.

We are who we are—grandmas. And it's fun!

> *For you, O LORD, have made me glad by your*
> *work; at the works of your hands I sing for joy.*
>
> **Psalm 92:4**

January 17   Listening

Our own kids successfully avoided listening to us as much as possible.
Now that they are parents they listen intently to all we say to their children, our grandchildren.

> *Let your speech always be gracious, seasoned*
> *with salt, so that you may know how you ought*
> *to answer everyone.*
>
> **Colossians 4:6**

January 18   Mirrors

I don't deny my age; I admit I'm getting older. Occasionally, however, when I unexpectedly catch my image in the mirror, I'm surprised. That reflection does not reveal the complete me.

Inside of me remains a bit of a young, wide-eyed girl marveling at the life that awaits; and an insecure teenager seeking acceptance; and an energetic young adult ready to conquer worlds; and a new mother reveling at the mystery of birth; and....

I am a living relic of me as I was each day of my entire life. I am a complex composite of each experience, each thought and fear, each dream and prayer, each encounter with the world and humanity and God.

Somehow, all this is masked with wrinkles, time-worn skin, and grey hair.

> *For the LORD does not see as mortals see; they look on the outward appearance, but the LORD looks on the heart.*
>
> **1 Samuel 16:7**

January 19   Grand-Times

The time a grandmother spends with a grandchild is a grand-time!

The grand-time may have a domestic setting, with activities like baking cookies or making applesauce or canning pickles, cutting grass or raking leaves or gardening.

It may be a craft and hobby-time: woodworking, crocheting, drawing, painting, model building, cake decorating or collecting dolls, stamps, cards or coins.

It may be a nature trip: birding, fishing, taking photos or sighting constellations, collecting mushrooms or wildflowers or rocks or shells.

It may have a work setting: a business, office, factory, farm, forest; a truck, car, train, plane.

It may be an outing: circus, park, library, zoo, church, museum.

It may be a vacation place: a cabin, resort, hotel, campsite.

No matter what the setting or activity, whether working or playing or praying or storytelling or reading or talking or just "being," the time with a grandchild is a grand-time.

> *Do not deprive yourself of a day's enjoyment; do*
> *not let your share of desired good pass by you.*
>
> Sirach 14:14

January 20   Our "Dailys"

We grandmas have our daily chores, our daily reading, our daily exercise, our daily prayers, our daily vitamins and medicines.

But we mustn't forget our daily affirmations:

I am a loving person and I recognize love in others.

The Holy Spirit is guiding me and my family.

I forgive others, and I forgive myself.

I am at peace in God's love.

Today I begin a new life in Christ.

God's blessings are with me all the days of my life.

. . .

. . .

. . .

> *Be transformed by the renewing of your minds.*
>
> Romans 12.2

January 21   Playfulness

One accepted indication that a child is growing up is the abandonment of playthings like sand, mud, stones, construction paper, crayons, markers, sticks, blocks....

However, the reality may be that what we regard as maturity is actually the anesthetizing of the imaginations of our children.

We replace their glittering vision of the world with the prosaic view of a too-practical adulthood. We mistake their exuberance for emotional instability and rush to bury it in sophistication. We smother their creativity with righteousness and replace openness with selectively directed prejudice. We gasp at their truthfulness and train them to conform. We replace their natural wisdom—their understanding of the spirit of the law—with our obsession for the letter of the law.

Only then do we declare them mature.

What we need in this staid adult world are more creative solutions to our problems, more joyous trust in others, more natural wisdom, more truthfulness, and many more spontaneous acts of love.

That's why we are to become like little children.

> *(Jesus) said, "Truly I tell you, unless you change and become like children, you will never enter the kingdom of heaven."*
>
> **Matthew 18:3**

January 22   Reason for Living

It is through the experience of being loved that we are formed and changed and uplifted.

It is through the experience of loving that we find our reason for living.

I am the LORD, *I have called you in righteousness, I have taken you by the hand and kept
you; I have given you as a covenant to the people, a light to the nations.*

Isaiah 42:6

January 23   "Sacrificing"

P arents do not make "sacrifices" for their children.
    A parent, when confronted with a choice between some-
thing of benefit to the child and something of benefit to the
parent, often makes the decision in favor of the child. The reason
is simple: The parent's joy of nurturing combined with the satisfaction of seeing the child's happiness exceed that of any other possible choice. That's why it isn't a "sacrifice."

When children understand this they are released from burden-
some obligations to their parents for making "sacrifices" for them.

However, with this understanding may come a feeling of being
overwhelmed as the children comprehend, for the first time, the ex-
tent of their parents' love.

We love because he first loved us.

1 John 4:19

January 24   The Shaker

W ith extreme ease we can overlook the possibility that
    when the foundations of our lives are being shaken or
    destroyed it may be God who is doing the shaking!
*When they had prayed, the place in which they
were gathered together was shaken; and they*

were all filled with the Holy Spirit and spoke the word of God with boldness.

Acts 4:31

January 25   Someday

Someday" we're going to have a mother-daughter lunch date.

"Someday" we're going to write our family history.

"Someday" we're going to go on a weekend retreat.

"Someday" we're going to tell our children how much we love them.

"Someday" we're going to do a family tree for the grandkids.

"Someday...."

The calendar contains Mon-days, Tues-days, Wednes-days, Thurs-days, Fri-days, Satur-days, Sun-days, but no Some-days.

What has been is what will be, and what has been done is what will be done.

Ecclesiastes 1:9

January 26   Successful Parents

Defining "successful parents" has become increasingly difficult in today's complex world.

Not too many years ago a mother might point with pride to her six children, all of whom held responsible positions in the community. Nowadays she remains silent, for fear time will prove she nurtured a half-dozen workaholics who are unable to enter into close, personal relationships.

Another mother hesitates to boast of her daughter who survived the teenage period with a minimum of trauma, for fear that the same daughter might undergo a severe midlife crisis because of an unresolved issue from adolescence.

Today's grandparents, aware of the depressingly large number of divorces among the long-married, no longer can regard their offspring as safely married or securely settled.

Our newly evolving awareness of the human psyche includes the realization that we need to refrain from assessing the success of parenthood, at least until the biblical third and fourth generations.

> *If you choose, you can keep the commandments,*
> *and to act faithfully is a matter of your own*
> *choice.*

Sirach 15:15

January 27   A Test of Faith

One of the great challenges of parenthood is recognizing that God's plan for our offspring may not be identical to our plan.

Often it is easier to recognize the workings of the Holy Spirit in anyone else in the entire world than in our own young. We look at the neighbor whose life has been filled with "wrong" decisions and we say, "God writes straight with crooked lines." In reference to the teenager down the street, we comment, "She's testing her freedom." And then there's that second cousin of ours who has gone through career changes, experimental lifestyles, and a series of identity crises, and we confidently predict, "Someday he'll find himself."

But our own child or grandchild?

It requires tremendous faith to recognize that the person standing before us is a unique child of God with a role to fulfill which we may not be able to direct. It might even be a role which we neither recognize nor understand. Yet we are called to acknowledge the Holy Spirit's promptings in our offspring and to reaffirm our belief in prayer, in acceptance, and in love.

The fruit of the Spirit is love, joy, peace, patience, kindness, generosity, faithfulness, gentleness, and self-control.

Galatians 5:22-23

January 28   Unexpected Pleasures

For as far back as I can remember, I heard about the joys of having grandchildren—and I have not been disappointed!

But what has come as an unexpected pleasure is the joy of seeing my child as a parent.

How reassuring it is to witness the development of my child as a learning, groping, committed, interested, faithful parent.

How reassuring it is to see carried over to yet one more generation the good that I as a mother was able to do.

How encouraging it is to see my parental deficits corrected by my child with regard to my grandchild.

How profoundly satisfying it is to watch the growth of the love of my child for my grandchild.

(The righteous) are ever giving liberally and lending, and their children become a blessing.

Psalm 37:26

January 29   "Where Are You, Grandma?"

Where are you, Grandma?" my grandchildren call.

Where am I?

I may be in the kitchen, baking cookies, or in the boardroom, chairing a meeting.

I may be in the classroom, teaching kindergarten, or in the science lab, pursuing a long-postponed degree, or in the university auditorium, conducting a graduate seminar.

I may be in a rocking chair, cuddling my newest grandchild, or in a courtroom, presenting my summary argument.

I may be in the nursing home, presiding at a prayer service or caring for the infirm there or lying in one of the beds, longing for visitors.

I may be on the golf course or the picket line; I may be in the welfare line or the volunteer line; I may be on the assembly line or in the dance line; I may be praying or crafting or dusting or singing or traveling.

I may even be at the computer, writing a book.

I, Grandma, am *everywhere*!

> *I am going to send an angel in front of you, to guard you on the way and to bring you to the place that I have prepared.*

Exodus 23:20

January 30   "I Am"

"I am" are magic words; they are the *abracadabra* used by all of us.

What we say we are, we are in the process of becoming even more. Every time I describe myself—in words or thoughts—with an "I am" statement, I become that ever more deeply.

When I talk to others I have an opportunity to present them with a description of themselves that might provide them with words to form their own "I am" pronouncements. I must choose carefully these word-gifts I offer others.

"I am" are magic words. They can retard growth, dissipate enthusiasm, curtail creativity, undermine self-confidence.

The magic words "I am" can also bring about joy and renewed vigor and insight and understanding and even miracles!

God said to Moses, "I AM WHO I AM....This is my name forever, and this my title for all generations."

Exodus 3:14-15

January 31   "What's New?"

Years ago, when I met an acquaintance I hadn't seen for a time, I would ask specific questions. I might inquire:
How's your husband (wife)?
Are your brother and his fiancée married yet?
Is your sister in college?
Are the kids still living at home?
But that was at a time before the burgeoning divorce rate (even of the long-married) and the increasing number of young people leading very convoluted lives and the high rate of single parenting and the consideration of significant others and the modern approach to same sex marriages and the increase in blended families and the use of sperm banks and the hiring of surrogate mothers and....

After a number of extremely embarrassing encounters, I undertook a new approach. Now, when I meet an acquaintance I haven't seen in a long time, I confidently ask, "What's new?"

If any of you is lacking in wisdom, ask God,
who gives to all generously and ungrudgingly,
and it will be given you.

James 1:5

February 1 — Always "Mom"

I certainly admit that parenthood is forever. Once a mom, always a mom; once a grandma, always a grandma.

But what I want to know is, does it have to be *only* a mom? Or *only* a grandma?

Is it possible for my offspring to view me as other than one defined by the parenting role?

Do they ever wonder what I did or what I was before motherhood? Do they realize that it is possible for me to have a life outside of the family?

Can't they see that having a self-image that extends beyond parenting does not indicate rejection of my mothering role? Can't they see that the more fulfilled I am as a person, the better parent and grandparent I am?

Do they ever view me as a person with talents and abilities other than those involved in parenting? Do they recognize my responsibilities—to myself, to others, to the world—to use those God-given talents?

Can they see me as a unique individual apart from "Mom" and "Grandma"?

> *Sleeper, awake!*
>
> **Ephesians 5:14**

February 2 — Adolescence

We often greet the adolescence of our grandchildren with less than grateful enthusiasm. This stage of development is easier to survive, however, when we remember that confrontation and rebellion are necessary in each child's struggle for independence. Our own children survived it; our grandchildren will too.

The emergence of a butterfly from its restrictive cocoon has its moments of struggle, fear and peril. This stressfully exciting time requires deep, committed faith in the Creator and in the creature-in-transition. But what joy there is in seeing the winged creature that finally emerges.

The emergence of a young adult from the cocoon of adolescence also has its moments of struggle, fear and peril. This stressfully exciting time requires deep, committed faith in the Creator and in the creature-in-transition. But what joy there is in seeing the beauty and character of the new adult-friend who finally emerges!

> *I was overjoyed to find some of your children walking in the truth.*
>
> 2 John 4

February 3   Birthday Party

I n our family," a friend said, "children were never allowed to have birthday parties. We could have parties to celebrate the anniversary of our birth—but that was different. My grandma believed the focus of a birthday celebration was the marvelous gift of life itself.

"Celebrating a person's birthday was honoring that person's whole life, and so we thanked God for all the blessings that person brought to our world. Therefore, to expect friends to bring gifts demeaned the main reason for the celebration.

"So when Grandma celebrated her birthday she was the one doing the giving. She gave presents to the rest of the family and to her close friends, and invited us to celebrate her life with her.

"My grandmother gave wonderful parties; she loved people and celebrations and life!"

> *And now bless the God of all, who everywhere works great wonders, who fosters our growth*

from birth, and deals with us according to his mercy.

Sirach 50:22

February 4   Competition

Sometimes we need to be reminded that the most important aspects of life are not inherently competitive:
Love is without measure or limit, for all love comes from God, who is unbounded love.
Parenting—including grandparenting—is not a contest with neighbors or relatives or friends.
The value of each and every person is without measure, and therefore cannot be equated.
Sanctity is noncompetitive.
Don't our grandchildren deserve a nonthreatening, noncompetitive environment?

Some are last who will be first, and some are first who will be last.

Luke 13:30

February 5   Just Coping

Coping is often unrecognized as an important and distinctively meritorious virtue. No one would say "She's *just* courageous" or "She's *just* charitable." But "She's *just* coping" is a common expression.

When life brings us fulfillment we have no need of faith. When we experience success we don't need hope. When parenthood and job or profession and volunteer work are all triumphant ventures, we need not seek help from others or from God. It is only when life does not bring fulfillment, success or triumph that we become reacquainted with the virtue of coping.

Coping is a testament to the presence of other virtues such as perseverance, commitment, faithfulness, hope. Thus, "I am coping" is an affirmation of life, a statement of faith. It is a courageous declaration of victory made while still engaged in battle.

Since coping is an all-consuming occupation, we are often unaware at the time of insights gained and virtuous deeds performed. Only hindsight indicates how much spiritual progress we made during a time of "just coping."

> *It is good to give thanks to the Lord,*
> *to sing praises to your name, O Most High;*
> *to declare your steadfast love in the morning,*
> *and your faithfulness by night.*

Psalm 92:1-2

February 6   Saints

I am surrounded by saints—by people who respond wholeheartedly to God's call to holiness. I affirm and support all the many noble people who really do bring Christ to earth today:

Those unselfish grandparents who have undertaken the raising of their grandchildren;

Those faithful spouses who care for their mate with Alzheimer's or Parkinson's or AIDS or cancer or...;

Those foster parents who provide homes for needy kids;

Those respite care people who supply relief to caregivers;

Those who teach, who work with, who care for the young;

Those who minister to the elderly, the people with handicaps, the poor;

Those who practice gospel values in the marketplace;

Those who love enthusiastically, unstintingly, recklessly, passionately.

Bear one another's burdens, and in this way you
will fulfill the law of Christ.

Galatians 6:2

February 7   I Have a Dream

Each year at this time we are reminded of the words, the life, and the death of Martin Luther King, Jr. Often quoted is his "I Have a Dream" speech.

I too have a dream. I dream of the day when children will have to consult a dictionary for the meaning of such archaic terms as:

> racism
> poverty
> bigotry
> war
> discrimination
> homophobia
> sexism
> prejudice.

Until such a dream is the vision of all, we shall live in a world where nightmares too often become the reality.

> *Jerusalem, Jerusalem, the city that kills the*
> *prophets and stones those who are sent to it!*

Luke 13:34

February 8   Detachment

Vicky is one of my mentors. One day I admired a message button that she was wearing.

"Do you like it?" Vicky asked.

"Yes. It really speaks to me," I answered.

Undoing the clasp, she said, "I have enjoyed it; now it's yours." And she handed it to me.

Vicky never seeks more than she needs today; she never owns more than she can use now. She does not hoard, for someone else may need whatever had been placed in her keeping. When bounty comes her way she immediately distributes the excess.

While her life exemplifies many things, she personifies for me the rare virtue of detachment.

> *Whoever has two coats must share with anyone*
> *who has none; and whoever has food must do*
> *likewise.*

Luke 3:11

February 9   Free!

J uggle home and work, family and friends?
Been there; done that!
Balance school and church and community involvement?
Been there; done that!

Function on multilevels simultaneously with different ages of kids and competing entanglements?

Been there; done that!

Organize, assist, deal with, work in, help with, publicize, set up, clean up (*fill in the blank*)?

Been there; done that!

Handle and survive crises, emergencies, disasters?

Been there; done that!

There comes a time in life when we grandmas realize we don't have to prove anything to anyone anymore.

> *For freedom Christ has set us free. Stand firm,*
> *therefore, and do not submit again to a yoke of*
> *slavery.*

Galatians 5:1

A favorite Hebrew Scripture story is about Elijah and the starving widow and her son. After Elijah had miraculously provided food for them, they offered him the shelter of their poor home; each was grateful for the friendship.

But then tragedy struck; the son—the widow's only child—died. Unable to comfort her, Elijah approached the son's body. Praying from the depths of his being, he flung himself upon the body, placing his mouth against the stilled youth's mouth. Gasping deeply, he breathed, again and again, into the inert form. And the boy "awakened" (1 Kings 17).

How can we, who are tediously familiar with Scripture's life-restoring miracles, appreciate the prophet's faith? For Elijah knew nothing of those miraculous events yet to occur.

He asked God to perform a "new" miracle, for history had never recorded such a wonder. Never before, to our knowledge or to his, had a person been restored to life. As hopeless as the situation appeared, Elijah maintained his belief in God's goodness.

That's our kind of faith! It does not matter that what we grandmothers are praying for has never previously occurred. We are called to have the faith that believes in all kinds of miracles, even "new" ones.

For nothing will be impossible with God.

Luke 1:37

February 11   Guarantees

F or years I watched Mark and Brian as they endured their scarring years as children of alcoholics. Eventually Mark left home, entered the service and then went to college, married a fine young woman, had a family, and became very involved in an alcohol-free life. Brian's story was a continuing saga of life on the downward spiral, composed of failures, opportunities missed and always the ever-present specter of alcohol abuse.

Each of them, when asked about his life, gives the same answer: "Considering my background, what would you expect?"

There is no guarantee in the parenting business, no method that assures a specific result. Such a thing cannot exist, for it would contradict the realities of free will, divine mercy, the power of love, miracles, the efficacy of prayer, conversion. It would even contradict life itself, for change is one of life's characteristics. If the individual's right to change were denied, there would be no mystery, no need for faith, no tears of joy. There would be no heroes or stories.

Our offspring must always have the freedom to err—a God-given right—along with the freedom to repent, to change, to participate in the miracles of love. That's why there are no guarantees in parenting.

> *God did not give us a spirit of cowardice, but rather a spirit of power and of love and of self-discipline.*
>
> **2 Timothy 1:7**

February 12   Going Alone

I t isn't a matter of not being *able* to do it; nor is it that I'm *afraid* to do it. It's just that some things were not meant to be experienced alone.

Some events and outings significantly decrease in enjoyment when done solo. Music and dance presentations are designed for parties of more than one; art exhibits are more enjoyable when they can be discussed along the way; lectures and movies increase tremendously in enrichment when they can be reviewed later with another; travel is lonely when solitary; even food is tastier and digestion is aided when meals are not private experiences.

It's not that I can't go alone. It's just that there is no such thing as a *party* of one!

> *Be strong and courageous; do not be frightened*
> *or dismayed, for the LORD your God is with you*
> *wherever you go.*

Joshua 1:9

February 13   Homilies

Of the many, many homilies I've heard, how many do I remember? Even though I have been privileged to hear some very gifted speakers, I must confess that I can recall very few.

So often, sermons and homilies do not necessarily "speak" to us. Nor do they necessarily "speak" to our young.

The way in which we live our lives is most often influenced by what we saw our parents and grandparents do. And what our youth do now and will do in the future is greatly determined by what we, their elders, do. Examples speak louder than words.

Preachers carry prestige and recognition; they have degrees and titles and positions of prominence. But when we look at reality, parents and grandparents have the real power.

> *Thus you will know them by their fruits.*

Matthew 7:20

February 14   Valentine's Day

Today's focus is love; so it's appropriate to consider some "love notes":

Childhood is characterized by the need to be loved;
Maturity is characterized by the need to love.

Love has the potential of performing miracles,
For love itself is a miracle.

Love is lots of little things—
And also the Biggest Thing.
> **Let us love, not in word or speech, but in truth
> and action.**

1 John 3:18

February 15 Jellybeans

Gourmet jellybeans?"

"Yes, Grandmamam! Take one at a time. Here, try this one."

"Just one jellybean?"

"Just one! Now put it in your mouth and close your eyes. Roll the jellybean gently around in your mouth. Got it?"

"Hmmmm."

"Now gently bite into it; savor the flavor. Concentrate on that jellybean—really become one with it."

"Hmmmm."

"Well, Grandmamam, can you guess what it is?"

"Could it possibly be...popcorn?"

> **O taste and see that the LORD is good!**

Psalm 34:8

February 16 Labeling

I located the permanent marker and name labels. The table was already piled with clothes and personal items. Reluctantly, I began the familiar task of labeling all those articles.

Over the years I have done this many times. For my own kids, there were the labeling sessions preceding kindergarten, scout trips, sport and cheerleading camps, the military, college. For my grandkids, I help with labeling preceding day care and school excursions.

How different this is, I thought to myself as I marked my mother's name on the things she would take with her to the nursing home.

> *Again I saw that under the sun the race is not to the swift, nor the battle to the strong, nor bread to the wise, nor riches to the intelligent, nor favor to the skillful; but time and chance happen to them all.*

Ecclesiastes 9:11

February 17   Ever-Learning

We rejoice—and rightly so—whenever a child learns a valuable lesson, acquires a skill, achieves a goal. From first steps to cap-and-gown, we encourage and praise.

Yet as we, their elders, learn more about the human condition, we often experience not joy, but guilt. So often our understanding of humanity and relationships seems to come late with regard to our own actions and words. We hear ourselves saying, "If I had only known...." or "I never realized how important it is to...." Our learning often comes packaged with regret.

Yet guilt and regret do nothing constructive for us. Rather, they sap our strength and prevent us from wholeheartedly devoting ourselves to the present. As we continue to learn about our offspring and ourselves, we need to celebrate our newly discovered insights and knowledge just as we celebrated the milestones of our children.

Learning is an integral part of life, even during grandparent-hood. We are all ever-learning!

> *For the LORD gives wisdom;*
> *from his mouth come knowledge and under-*
> *standing.*

Proverbs 2:6

February 18   Midnight

Midnight and those slow-paced hours of darkness that follow have a special place in parental life.

Rising for infant feedings is the initiation into a nocturnal society. Membership is renewed with each lingering dark hour spent by a sick child's bedside. Full lifetime membership is bestowed upon those who have spent drawn-out hours waiting for the familiar sounds of a car door and a teenage footstep, while thoughts of alcohol and drugs and sex and accidents run rampant. Yet those worries can be instantly wiped out with a "Hi, Dad. What are you doing up?" or "What's the matter, Mom, couldn't you sleep?"

As our sleeplessness continues, we are united not only with other parents but also with all those in the Church who did, do and will observe the canonical hours of the divine office, rising in darkest night to pray. So we too might heed the call to participate fully in our clandestine society by rising, lighting a candle, and praying. It has been said that we cannot touch a flower without moving a star; surely then, to rise up in the darkest of night to light a candle brightens the earth and lights the way for someone, somewhere.

> *The LORD is my light and my salvation;*
> *whom shall I fear?*

Psalm 27:1

February 19   Power of Music

We soothe the crying baby
with nursery rhymes and games, songs and lullabies.
We distract the rambunctious toddler
with nursery rhymes and games, songs and lullabies.
We entertain the sick youngster
with nursery rhymes and games, songs and lullabies.
We divert the discouraged adolescent
with nursery rhymes and games, songs and lullabies.
We revive the adult's child-within
with nursery rhymes and games, songs and lullabies.
We recall the oldster's past
with nursery rhymes and games, songs and lullabies.
We connect all of time
with nursery rhymes and games, songs and lullabies.

> *And whenever the evil spirit from God came*
> *upon Saul, David took the lyre and played it*
> *with his hand, and Saul would be relieved and*
> *feel better, and the evil spirit would depart from*
> *him.*

1 Samuel 16:23

February 20   Names

What do I call myself? How do I refer to myself when talking with others? Perhaps even more important, how do I refer to myself when talking to myself?
Are my names for myself affirming ones? Are they empowering names? Are they names that identify my God-given giftedness, my

chosen-ness?

How do I name others? The individuals in my family, my neighbors, my coworkers? Other groups of people? Other races, nationalities, religious groups?

Do these names convey respect and honor? Do they recognize the Spirit of God which resides in each of us?

Throughout Scripture much emphasis is placed upon the importance of the names of people.

They are no less important today.

> *It is I, the LORD, the God of Israel, who call you*
> *by your name.*

Isaiah 45:3

February 21   Our Friend

One of our greatest needs is to have a close friend—other than our mate. Our husband, who may well be our closest friend, puts responsibilities on us, has expectations of us, makes demands of us.

What a treasure to have another good friend! We need someone who accepts us as we are, who listens without judging, who flatters our ego when it is on the verge of withering away, who strokes our personality the right way, who builds us up when we are failing.

A true friend will listen to our anguish at the waywardness of one of our young without making us feel ashamed.

But perhaps an even more severe test, a true friend will listen to our exuberant declarations of the virtues and accomplishments of our offspring, and—rejecting both jealousy and envy—will joyously celebrate them with us!

> *Some friends play at friendship but a true friend*
> *sticks closer than one's nearest kin.*

Proverbs 18:24

February 22   Wonderful Are God's Works!

I give thanks to our ever-creating God
> for you, my grandchild.
While you were an infant in your mother's womb
> God knit you.
I give thanks
> that you are fearfully, wonderfully made.
The Spirit most holy knows you;
God is familiar with all your ways—
> knowing when you sit down and when you rise up.
Behind and before you
> God hems you in and guides you;
Your journeys and rest and actions
> are all written in God's book.
Wherever you go is in the Spirit,
> for God is everywhere!
God's right hand holds you fast.
At the end of your days
> God shall still be with you.
Wonderful are God's works!
> **_I praise you, for I am fearfully and wonderfully made._**

Psalm 139:14

February 23   Reality

What is *reality*?
Our discussion group spent several sessions considering the meaning of reality. Our consensus, after hours of discussion, was neither a metaphysical nor a philosophical definition, but rather a meaning culled from our experience: Reality is

what we think it is.

We make our own reality; reality is inside us. We may think that we live in that ever-expanding world outside of us, but that is not where we experience life. We live in the world of our minds and hearts.

We control the "weather" of that inner world by choosing which aspects of life we allow to influence us; we control the "scenery" and "environment" of that inner world by the thoughts which we allow to reside there.

It has been said that the happiness of our lives is dependent upon the quality of our thoughts. How powerful is the reality of my mind and heart and soul!

> *You desire truth in the inward being;*
> *therefore teach me wisdom in my secret heart.*
>
> **Psalm 51:6**

February 24   Child Sacrifice

The story of Abraham and Isaac reminded the ancient Hebrews that they were to reject absolutely child sacrifice. They recognized in the angel's words the moral triumph of Yahweh's worship over that of their neighbors, who practiced human sacrifice to their gods. They, the descendents of Abraham and Sarah, were to be different.

Unfortunately, we, their spiritual heirs, often continue to worship gods who demand child sacrifice—gods like Power, Greed, Convenience, Materialism, Self-interest.

Millions of children, although granted life, are deprived of the fulfillment of that life. Many suffer because we adults are too busy or distracted to nurture them. There are children who endure abuse at the hands of those who are supposed to care for them. The homeless in our country include multitudes of children and families. Nearly one in every four children under the age of six is growing up in poverty.

These are frightening statistics. They paint a picture as horrible as that of Abraham and Isaac. Child sacrifice was forbidden centuries ago. We cannot condone it now.

> *We were gentle among you, like a nurse tenderly caring for her own children.*
>
> 1 Thessalonians 2:7

February 25   Sex Education

The sex education of a child begins before the baby's birth, as the yet-to-be-born child hears the voices of Mom and Dad, senses their touches.

Sex education continues with the choices of baby clothes and nursery decorations, the toys in the bassinet, the nursery rhymes and songs and games.

Sex education continues with all that surrounds the child: playthings, books and stories, family models and mentors, the church's teachings and the church's models, media input, society's contributions.

The entire environment communicates, develops, reinforces attitudes toward sex, sexual mores, sexual roles.

The question is not *whether* there will be sex education; the question is *what kind*?

> *So God created humankind in his image, in the image of God he created them; male and female he created them. God blessed them, and God said to them "Be fruitful and multiply...." God saw everything that he had made, and indeed, it was very good.*
>
> Genesis 1:27-28, 31

February 26   Compassion

S orrow and pain, tragedy and heartache, are elements of the mystery of life.

"Why?" we ask.

And, almost as often, there is no answer.

I can recall quite vividly one lonely morning, following the oh-so-long night after one of our teenagers had run away. In the midst of the worry came a visitor. This mother sat with me as we waited together for the phone to ring or my child to appear.

"I often wondered," she said to me, "when my own son ran away, why this had to happen. But perhaps the reason is that now, though I have no words of wisdom to give you, I do know that I should be here to wait with you. Perhaps that is sufficient answer to my why."

Sometimes, the only benefit from an ordeal seems that we then have the understanding and compassion to sit with another in silence, knowing that words are unnecessary.

> *Where two or three are gathered in my name, I am there among them.*

Matthew 18:20

February 27   The Tablecloth

Y esterday, just *yesterday*, I got rid of a tablecloth with a history. No, not a history of its use for family meals or holiday festivities, for it never, during its long life, came in contact with a table!

The tablecloth's history began many years ago when I started embroidering it. However, I never finished it. I really intended to complete it, but my life became filled with kids and so much busyness.

Through several family moves the tablecloth was packed and unpacked. Then I buried it in the cedar chest, its presence periodically rediscovered whenever I was searching there. But even when it wasn't visible, I knew its location and half-finished condition. There it lay throughout those years of births and First Holy Communions and Confirmations, graduations and marriages and another generation of births.

Eventually I moved it to the sewing drawer where it would greet me with an unspoken "Finish me!" But somehow—for whatever reasons—I never did.

Finally, after all these years, the never-used, never-completed tablecloth was thrown out—and I am wonderfully, delightfully relieved!

> *(There is) a time to keep, and a time to throw away.*
>
> Ecclesiastes 3:6

February 28   Test-Obsession

Some school counselors, teachers, administrators, and parents, are prone to test-obsession. An over-emphasis on I.Q. tests, aptitude tests, achievement tests, and college entrance exams causes people to regard test results as the scientific version of fortune telling updated with divinely ordained prophetic instrumentation.

But tests are limited in their capacity to predict future achievement. They do not take into account determination or motivation; they cannot assess the impact of maturity or the effects of perseverance and boldness and inspiration; they ignore what can be accomplished through cooperation; nor do they measure the power of love.

Throughout time God has, in wisdom divine, chosen those who rank low according to human evaluation for the important tasks in salvation history.

> *Then Judith said to them, "Listen to me. I am*
> *about to do something that will go down*
> *through all generations of our descendants."*
>
> Judith 8:32

February 29   Awareness Day

This day is Awareness Day.

This day I am aware of the many "extras" in my life.

This day I am aware of all the beauty and joy and laughter that surround me, that I may enter into that fullness of life, making it mine.

This day I am aware of the sorrow and suffering that surround me, that I may wholeheartedly respond to those in need.

This day I am aware of graces in abundance and of God who is the source of all that is good and beautiful.

This day I am aware of God's presence and love. I listen to God's voice speaking to me—through the Spirit dwelling in me, through the Spirit dwelling in those around me.

This day, which unfortunately comes only once every four years, I am aware of everything!

> *You have made known to me the ways of life;*
> *you will make me full of gladness with your*
> *presence.*
>
> Acts 2:28

March 1   Aches 'n Pains

Focusing so many of my thoughts on ill-health doesn't make me feel better. Instead, those negative thought-habits reinforce all my limitations; the aches 'n pains remain, intensified and magnified by my attention.

Right now I am determined to focus my thoughts on good health, on my unimpaired abilities, on the enjoyment of life, on the mercy and goodness of God.

As I think about my many blessings, I begin to feel better.

As I think positively about physical well-being, I feel better.

As I breathe deeply, I take on wellness and healing—and I feel even better.

As I relax my mind and emotions and spirit, I take comfort in God's indwelling presence—and I am better.

> *A cheerful heart is a good medicine,*
> *but a downcast spirit dries up the bones.*
>
> **Proverbs 17:22**

March 2   Blessings

A blessing can take the form of a person, a thing, a thought, a word, an event.

The Creator, delighting in humor best understood from an eternal perspective, is unsurpassed in disguising blessings—often camouflaging them as crosses, challenges, disappointments, defeats, and unanswered prayers.

It is only with the 20/20 vision of hindsight that blessings can be recognized unerringly.

O the depth of the riches and wisdom and
knowledge of God! How unsearchable are his
judgments and how inscrutable his ways!

Romans 11:33

March 3   Balance

Deep down, somewhere at gut-level, I'm convinced there is symmetry in life.

I can't prove it, of course, but I keep thinking that if we could pile the various opposing ingredients of life on balance scales, the two sides would be in equilibrium.

The joys would balance with the sorrows; the busy times and the boring times, the togetherness and the loneliness, the mountain-top experiences and the deep-valley traumas, the crises and the contentment would balance.

But if this is so, I still wonder why so much of life is spent in the extremes of too much or too little, too early or too late, too noisy or too quiet, too few or too many....

Why can't more of life be lived harmoniously in a state of equilibrium?

Even in laughter the heart is sad,
and the end of joy is grief.

Proverbs 14:13

March 4   Anointing

Long before anyone ever heard of the human need for bonding, long before anyone studied the importance of touching, there was anointing. Individuals who had been singled out from the clan were signed with aromatic ointment; the transference of authority took place with the touching of oils; accomplishments were recognized with such rites; final farewells were conferred with sweet-smelling balms. In the Hebrew Scriptures the word "Messiah" means "anointed," for that ritual symbolized Yahweh's spirit being communicated to the chosen one.

Today we know that touch is the most fundamental sense. A baby experiences it while still in the womb, and no human ever ceases to need it. And so we adults anoint our young—with baby oil and healing ointments and salves, with perfumed liniments and lotions. We rub and massage and wipe and stroke and caress. Through touching we attempt to eliminate pain, sad memories, rejection; through the feel of skin against skin we communicate love and acceptance; through our physical contact with one another we transfer heritage and blessing, hope, faith and sacredness.

> *A woman came to (Jesus) with an alabaster jar*
> *of very costly ointment, and she poured it on his*
> *head as he sat at the table...."Truly I tell you,*
> *wherever this good news is proclaimed in the*
> *whole world, what she has done will be told in*
> *remembrance of her."*

Matthew 26:7,13

March 5 "Be Still!"

How often we have said it to our kids!
"Be still!"
How often we continue to say it to our grandkids!
"Be still!"
How often God says it to us!
"Be still!"

Now there was a great wind, so strong that it was splitting mountains and breaking rocks in pieces before the LORD, but the LORD was not in the wind; and after the wind an earthquake, but the LORD was not in the earthquake; and after the earthquake a fire, but the LORD was not in the fire; and after the fire a sound of sheer silence. When Elijah heard it, he wrapped his face in his mantle and went out and stood at the entrance of the cave.

1 Kings 19:11-13

March 6   Celebration

Celebrations are an integral part of family life.

There are, of course, the special occasions to commemorate—holidays and birthdays and times of transition. The most important reasons to celebrate, however, are nearly always present, awaiting only our recognition: celebration of life; celebration of hope; celebration of a lovely day; celebration of peace; celebration of family history; celebration of love.

It is amazing how little is needed for a grandma to transform a ho-hum day into a celebration: a fancy tablecloth and favorite dessert, an unexpected bunch of flowers, a lingering kiss or an enthusiastic bear hug, a surprise gift, a well-chosen greeting card, an unplanned visit, a prayer shared, a phone call to say "I love you."

Beloved, let us love one another, because love is from God.

1 John 4:7

March 7   Chocolate

In manner most reverent, my friend Helen presented me with the covered plate of goodies.

"I pass on to you," she said in hushed tones, "the wise words given to me long ago: There is absolutely nothing in life that receiving chocolate from a friend cannot make better."

> *For everything created by God is good, and*
> *nothing is to be rejected, provided it is received*
> *with thanksgiving.*
>
> **1 Timothy 4:4**

March 8   Conservation of Energy

Because of my age I feel entitled to be more selective in how I spend my time and energy.

Some tasks really do seem to take so much out of me. I'm convinced that one hour spent doing them shortens my life by three or four.

But other tasks are different. They energize me. Even though I may become physically tired, I am renewed and refreshed. I find joy in the work, satisfaction in the completed job, pride in the end result.

These are the tasks, the jobs, the volunteer work, the hobbies, the recreational activities that bring meaning to my very existence.

I'll take *these* assignments, thank you, and you can find someone else for all the others!

> *We have gifts that differ according to the grace*
> *given to us.*
>
> **Romans 12:6**

March 9   Counting Down

All our lives, we count down.

As little girls we counted down the days to our birthdays or to Christmas, to vacations or to special events. We've had school and graduation and prom and wedding countdowns.

And oh, those long count-downs involved in giving birth! And the many count-downs to the events of our kids' lives as we began counting anew.

Yet now one more important count-down emerges—that of the unknown number of the active days and years remaining before us.

We consider all the dreams and goals that we have postponed or not accomplished and ask, "If not now, when?" We review our accumulation of wisdom and experience and ask, "How can I now most effectively use my talents?" We evaluate our contributions to the world and ask, "What remains for me to do to help assure that this world is a better place because I have visited here?"

As we elder, this count-down stimulates our plans and galvanizes our activity; we are energized into action one more time.

Now is the acceptable time!

2 Corinthians 6:2

March 10   Diary

How wonderful it must be to have the habit of diary-keeping. How interesting to be able to read your thoughts put on paper years ago. How fascinating to be able to look over all the various stages of your development and see your erratic maturing process.

I really wish I had kept a diary all my life. I wish I had entered all my feelings and fears, desires and prayers, joys and pains and transition times; I wish I now had those encapsulated word-pictures of life's dailyness.

But I didn't. And when my regret seems especially poignant one thought consoles me: I probably would not have recorded what was truly important.

Looking back, I have this nagging feeling that what I now remember—the thoughts and feelings that have endured from the past—is not what seemed significant at the occasion. Importance is often determined by the sieve of time; time both diminishes and magnifies; maturity evaluates with a different measure. Only what follows indicates the true value of what preceded.

But I still wish I had kept a diary.

> *Now write what you have seen, what is, and what is to take place after this.*
>
> **Revelation 1:19**

March 11   Dwelling Place

As the psalmist sings, "How lovely is your dwelling place, O Lord of Hosts."

And where is that dwelling place? Where does my Creator-God abide?

Not only everywhere but also within me.

Where does my Teacher and Friend and Savior dwell?

Not only everywhere but also within me.

Where does the Holy Spirit, the Dove of Creativity, the Fire of Passion dwell?

Not only everywhere but also within me.

Truly, how lovely am I, for my God dwells within me!

> *By this we know that we abide in him and he in us, because he has given us of his Spirit.*
>
> **1 John 4:13**

One of the most important duties—and greatest privileges—of being a mother and a grandmother, of being a friend, of being church, of being community is to empower.

Each of us is a gift from God to the world. So while we are here on earth we are to develop the talents within ourselves; we are to encourage and nurture the gifts of one another.

Empowering one another, compassionately and patiently and faithfully, is our function because we belong to a faith community. Empowering one another, energetically, graciously, gracefully, is our duty because we share in the priesthood of Christ. Empowering the next generation is our privileged mode of shaping the future.

During this time of Lent, this season when we focus on growth and life's direction and end-times, it is appropriate to renew our commitment to empowerment. The family of God needs the fulfillment of the potentials within each one of us, for that is how we bring forth the reign of God.

> *The kingdom of heaven is like yeast that a*
> *woman took and mixed in with three measures*
> *of flour until all of it was leavened.*

Matthew 13:33

Kim was a seriously ill child from Southeast Asia adopted into a large American family. Despite the love extended to him by his new family he remained emotionally detached. Kim's poor health required frequent hospitalization. "Visiting him in the hospital seemed like such a waste of time," his mother said.

"Sometimes we played games or I read to him, but usually I just sat there. Kim always seemed very far away, as though only his shadow had made the journey to this country.

"But the day before Kim was to have major surgery, I was sitting with this boy I didn't know, when he began speaking. No one knew his background or how much Kim himself could remember. That day he told me: When he was very young, his father abused him, before abandoning both Kim and his mother. Then his mother died. As Kim spoke, he reached out to me—and in that instance I realized that he was finally responding to our love. He had been terribly lonely, yet he preferred that to risking abandonment once again."

As Mother Teresa has reminded us, we are called to be faithful, not successful. Sometimes our faithfulness is rewarded—by an extended hand from a hospital bed or even the Nobel Peace Prize. But that is all secondary.

> *Now faith is the assurance of things hoped for,*
> *the conviction of things not seen.*

Hebrews 11:1

March 14 — Guidelines

I realize that times have changed—I don't need others to remind me of that. But have people themselves changed so much in the span of one generation?

I just do not understand the way my kids are raising my grandkids. It's as if all the guidelines have been removed—not just relocated, but abolished. Why don't these modern parents realize they aren't doing their children any favors by raising them to be above rule-keeping or ignorant of manners?

I really don't believe that society is strengthened or improved by individuals who don't respect laws and property, who are inconsiderate of others, who are noisy and self-indulgent.

Our world doesn't need more people who think they are the center of it.

> *Do not be deceived; God is not mocked, for you*
> *reap whatever you sow.*

Galatians 6:7

March 15   Being Happy

Once upon a time I thought that some people were happy because they had reason to be happy; I also thought that other people were unhappy because they had reason to be unhappy.

But that was when I was young. Now I've come to the realization that some people are never happy, while others, no matter what the circumstances, seem to be able to rise above those circumstances and find joy somewhere in their lives.

As a wise friend of mine observed, "Perhaps it is a special gift—that of being happy."

If so, it is a gift that can also be refused.

> *Happy is everyone who fears the LORD,*
> *who walks in his ways.*

Psalm 128:1

March 16   Going to Church

Why do we have to go to church, Grandma?" How many times I have answered that question.

"Dear, remember your birthday party last year when your big brother was away at college and couldn't attend?"

"Sure I do, Grandma. I really missed him."

"Well, going to church is a celebration. We celebrate God and we celebrate ourselves. And we—together—worship God in a public way.

"That celebration, called 'liturgy,' is lessened when even one member of our community isn't there. If I don't attend, that liturgy is diminished because I'm not there. If you don't attend, that liturgy is weakened because you're not there."

"But Grandma, I don't do anything special in the service."

"Oh but you do! You and I are very important. We are part of the assembly of believers. Our being there is a public act of faith, for our presence and participation support and inspire everyone else. We are important to each other and to the community's worship of God. If we don't go—you and I—our faith-family would miss us!"

> *Praise the LORD! Sing to the LORD a new song,*
> *his praise in the assembly of the faithful.*
>
> **Psalm 149:1**

March 17   The Tradition of Blessing

It's time for the annual inundation! Everywhere—on cards and mugs and plates and bookmarks—are poems and prayers carrying the notation: "An old Irish blessing."

But why should we non-Irish let the Irish (or, for that matter, the ordained) have a monopoly on blessings? Blessing one another is an ancient and hallowed part of our Judeo-Christian heritage, for blessing others is described numerous times in Scripture. Our faith is rich in this tradition of blessing.

We do not need anyone's permission to bless; we do not need authorization to ask God's grace to be bestowed on others.

Today I reclaim that oft-neglected tradition. Today I bless—and will continue to bless—my grandchildren, my family, those close to me, all who are in need, all whom I love.

> *All the women of Israel gathered to see (Judith),*
> *and blessed her.*

Judith 15:12

March 18   Holy Ground

"Someday," Vicky said smilingly, "we're going to put a sign on our door: TAKE OFF YOUR SHOES, FOR YOU ARE WALKING ON HOLY GROUND."

Vicky and David have transformed their home into a world-in-miniature with seventeen children of various races, colors, ethnic backgrounds, and handicaps. Refusing to be intimidated by lack of money, space, fancy furniture, prestige cars, and status clothing, they concentrate only on an abundance of love given generously to all who enter their home.

They have made a commitment to the vocation of parenthood. Their home is consecrated by acceptance—acceptance of different-hued kids; of unwanted kids; of a kidney-less kid dependent upon dialysis; of a kid with a gnome-like face, spunky spirit, and no arms; of a legally blind kid. Such acceptance surely has the power to make holy.

Food shared and stories told hallow their home, as do prayers and tears and hugs and forgiveness. Vicky and David deserve that sign, for their home is indeed holy space.

> *Surely the LORD is in this place!*

Genesis 28:16

March 19   The Idealism of Christianity

With age and experience we learn to recognize idealism. Idealism transcends the simplistic intent of the perfectionist who is committed to the complete achieving of goals, with compromise considered defeat. While such rigidity may occasionally result in success, it may also produce cynicism, pessimism or even despair.

Christianity is the idealism epitomized by our Creator, who did not abandon us in our waywardness. It is the idealism of a God who came to earth as one of us to teach us how to live; the idealism of a God who has never stopped loving or forgiving us; the idealism of a God whose spirit dwells within each of us.

Christianity is the idealism of very fallible human beings who recognize ultimate victory in seemingly hopeless situations. The sign by which we identify ourselves is itself a sign of ultimate degradation and seeming defeat, yet we Christians look at that cross and proclaim hope and victory and even love.

> *They crucified (Jesus), and with him two others, one on either side, with Jesus between them. Pilate also had an inscription written and put on the cross. It read, "Jesus of Nazareth, the King of the Jews."*

John 19:18-19

March 20   Job Application

Is there a more depressing task than filling out a job application? There's something about those forms that resembles an obituary—notations on my existence after the life blood of who I am has been removed.

How formidable it is to try to put on paper all the knowledge and insights and yes, wisdom, that I have gained over these many years. There's no category entitled "virtues developed" or "coping skills accrued"; there's no concise way to name the value of experience's informal education. I was never given a job description or had an interview for the most significant tasks of my life—I just did them.

In contrast, this job, this collection of responsibilities that exists on the other side of the application-and-hiring process, is just for money.

And when I complete this form, I then hand it over to someone young enough to be my own kid.

> ***Gray hair is a crown of glory;***
> ***it is gained in a righteous life.***

Proverbs 16:31

March 21   Listening Day

Today is Listening Day.

Today I listen to myself,
hearing myself as others might hear me.

Today I listen to my body,
hearing what it is telling me about how I live.

Today I listen to others,
hearing beyond words uttered to what the heart is saying.

Today I listen to God,
speaking through those around me,
and through the quiet voice within me.

Today is Listening Day.

> *Listen! I am standing at the door, knocking; if*
> *you hear my voice and open the door, I will*
> *come in to you and eat with you, and you with*
> *me.*

Revelation 3:20

March 22   The Message

I entered the small chapel and immediately stood transfixed. There before me was a crucifix such as I had never before seen. The form of the cross appeared inverted, for the crosspiece was placed low. The naked figure on the cross was female; her hands were bound together above her head and there nailed to the wood. Her feet were widely spread apart and each was nailed to the cross-piece.

The shocking, visual impact was one of intense vulnerability. The woman's secured hands spoke of the binding and restrictions commonly placed upon women. The soft, tender skin and curves of her body cried out for caressing, not torture; for giving life, not receiving assault. The exposed genital area and the coerced spread of her legs were unvoiced screams of violation.

Suddenly I saw, in a totally new dimension, the message of the gospel: Whatever we do to one another we do to Christ.

> *For this is the message you have heard from the*
> *beginning, that we should love one another.*

1 John 3:11

March 23 — OUT!

When the toddler wanders OUT!—out of the room, yard, car, house—the adult rushes off frantically in chase, fervently whispering prayers for the youngster's safety. When the teenager's answer to the question "Where are you going?" is "OUT!" the distraught adult turns to ardent prayer for the semi-adult's well-being.

Being around children has the effect of turning the subject of our prayers from ourselves to them.

> *Pray in the Spirit at all times in every prayer*
> *and supplication.*

Ephesians 6:18

March 24 — Patron Saints

The institutional Church has been miserly in presenting us canonized saints who were parents. The few exceptions are so unique that it is difficult for us to identify with them.

This scarcity of mentor married saints does not help us recognize our own calling to holiness.

We need to see the canonization of people who married, raised children, became grandparents, and throughout all this experienced the usual share of joys and heartaches within the sacramentality of everyday life.

We need to see the canonization of people who found God in the married state; who were able to regard parenthood as a religious vocation while up to their elbows in dirty diapers, leaky plumbing, broken bikes, overdue bills, ever-hungry kids, and demanding jobs; who brought to grandparenthood both love of God and love of people; who lived life in its fullest and deepest, holiest and heroic dimensions.

"All ye holy husbands and wives, pray for us."

"All ye holy mothers and fathers, pray for us."

"All ye holy grandmas and grandpas, pray for us."

> *Then I heard the voice of the LORD saying,*
> *"Whom shall I send, and who will go for us?"*
> *And I said, "Here am I; send me!"*

Isaiah 6:8

March 25   A Piece of the Truth

Now do you do that?" I asked, incredulous at the concept just described.

"Do what?" my new friend asked.

"You said you live in an intentional community which arrives at all decisions by consensus. What if everyone doesn't agree?"

"Oh, it's not easy! We always begin our discussions with prayer that we all remain open to the Holy Spirit. And, of course, we hope that everyone is able to put the community's good before his or her own preferences. Even then, that doesn't automatically bring about agreement.

"However, we believe that everyone has a piece of the truth. And so, as we discuss a topic, we really seek everyone's input to complete our understanding of the issues. Receiving every position as representing some aspect of the truth rather than labeling some of them as wrong or bad helps both the discussion and the decision-making.

"We each bring a piece of the truth to whatever we discuss. Over the years, our community has found that decision-making by consensus is worth the effort."

> *That they may all be one.*

John 17:21

March 26 — Praying

Bishop Desmond Tutu, when questioned about what he does in response to an enemy, said, "I pray for him. And I hope he knows it is a fearsome thing that I do!"

If it is a fearsome thing to pray for an enemy, how formidable, awesome, tremendously powerful an action we undertake when we pray for those we love.

> *Pray for the peace of Jerusalem:*
> *"May they prosper who love you.*
> *Peace be within your walls,*
> *and security within your towers."*
> *For the sake of my relatives and friends*
> *I will say, "Peace be within you."*
>
> **Psalm 122:6-8**

March 27 — Needed

No matter how little—or how much—I can do, I am needed.

Even if I cannot recognize my contributions to the world, I am needed.

Even when I cannot see the fruits of my labors, I am needed.

As I make my prayerful acts of faith in God, I include affirmations of my worthiness and important uniqueness in God's plans.

I am needed!

> *Do you not know that you are God's temple and*
> *that God's Spirit dwells in you?*
>
> **1 Corinthians 3:16**

March 28   Whirlwind

At times I feel at the mercy of outside events and other people, caught up in a whirlwind. It seems I have control over nothing.

But that's an illusion. Granted there are many aspects of life over which I have absolutely no control and other areas over which I should not attempt control. However, I do have control over my reactions—both to those outside events and to other people. I do have control over my thoughts.

No matter how forceful or intimidating that whirlwind, I can choose to think positive thoughts, affirming faith and love.

No matter how forceful or intimidating that whirlwind, I can choose to think positive thoughts, affirming confidence in my abilities and in the goodwill of others.

No matter how forceful or intimidating that whirlwind, I can choose to think positive thoughts, affirming trust in God's unending mercy and constant presence and guidance.

God is in the whirlwind too.

> *Now may the LORD of peace himself give you*
> *peace at all times in all ways.*
>
> **2 Thessalonians 3:16**

March 29   Receivers

We begin our existence as receivers, being given the gift of life from God and from our parents. Our survival is totally dependent upon others.

As we mature physically, emotionally and spiritually, our concerns are broadened; our focus becomes wider. With parenthood our concerns are directed toward others and we become givers.

And for some of us, as we age, life makes a complete circle and we become receivers once again.

If we have learned well from life, however, then we know that giving and receiving are but different facets of the same action. We have learned that the need to give can be as much a necessity as the need to receive. We have learned that what was originally the pride of giving yields to the humility of giving; and we have learned that the humility of receiving must yield to the pride of receiving. Both roles, being integral to the giving/receiving action, dignify the person. And the more nearly our giving and receiving balance each other in dignity and humility and responsibility, the more nearly we encompass the totality of love.

Let mutual love continue.

Hebrews 13:1

March 30 Consolation

We grandparents are living proof to the young of the Paschal Mystery, of dying and rising again.

We've survived the dying known as failure—and transformed it into learning.

We've survived the dying of completion—and gone on to begin anew.

We've survived the dying of wandering in life's valleys—and proceeded to climb other mountains.

We've survived the dying of disappointment—and rediscovered hope.

We've survived the dying of change—and learned adaptation.

We've survived the dying of sin—and tasted God's loving mercy.

We've survived the dying of regret—and experienced the reviving joy of the human spirit.

We've survived the dying of losing those close to us—and learned to appreciate life and friends all the more.

We look forward to surviving the dying known as dying—for we have faith in life everlasting.

> **The saying is sure: If we have died with him, we will also live with him.**
>
> **2 Timothy 2:11**

March 31 'Scopes

I used to think that only young kids mixed up *tele*scope and *micro*scope. But I'm now convinced it's a lifelong problem.

I find myself looking through the wrong end of the telescope at times, viewing events in my life through a distorted lens.

Or I think I'm taking the broad view of happenings when I'm actually looking through that microscope.

Only God, who doesn't need either 'scope, sees life clearly, in the perspective of eternity.

> **You will seek the LORD your God, and you will find him if you search after him with all your heart and soul.**
>
> **Deuteronomy 4:29**

April 1   Divine Comedian

God of Surprises,
 Maker of ducks and monkeys and kangaroos and koalas,
 Designer of galaxies,
Inventor of sex,
You are the Divine Incognito—
And you never cease to astound me!

And so, Comedian Most Holy,
in this comic-tragedy called life,
help me laugh.
Enable me to envision
beyond the present distractions
to your eternal joy.
Let me see in the times of boredom and loneliness
the presence of your humor.
Throughout my amusing journey from life-in-time
into life-in-eternity—
Help me laugh!

> *(God) will yet fill your mouth with laughter, and
> your lips with shouts of joy.*

Job 8:21

❧ ❧

April 2   Baptism Day

In the past, baptisms took place in darkened, empty churches,
 attended only by people involved in the ceremony or related to
 those awaiting baptism. It appeared to be a secret rite, an initiation into a clandestine organization whose members shunned
disclosure.

No more! Now on the day of baptism the entire congregation

shouts and sings our greeting: "Welcome! Welcome into our Christian community!" In welcoming this child into our faith, we also commit ourselves—parents and grandparents and friends and neighbors—to the nurturing of this child and all children.

And in response to this living gift from God, we sing our joy: "Praise be to God, the Creator of us all!" For if we cannot celebrate baptism, then what is there in this entire universe worth celebrating?

We rejoice at this new life; we rejoice at this new member of our Christian community; we rejoice in this community and in the larger Church; we rejoice in our treasury of traditions and liturgy and music and saints—past and present and to come.

> *This is the day that the LORD has made; let us rejoice and be glad in it.*
>
> **Psalm 118:24**

April 3   Answer the Question

My heart was aching—aching for a family devastated by a teenage suicide, aching for the hundreds of young people tearfully wondering "Why?"

During the vigil service I sat beside my grandson who shook with unshed tears. The young priest conducted a generic service, reading from his book or script without making eye contact with anyone in the chapel.

Never once did he acknowledge the agonized searching that showed on every face in that crowded room. Never once did he recognize the void that future time shall always have because of this incomplete life. Never once did he look compassionately at that sea of questioning countenances. Never once did he allow his humanity to emerge from behind the lectern.

I left the service angry—deeply, intensely angry.

That minister had a responsibility to address the question being asked by all those young people, a responsibility to them and to the

God and the Christian faith he represented. He had shirked that responsibility.

That man should have addressed the question everyone was asking—even if that answer was, "Who can know the mind of God?"

> *I lift up my eyes to the hills—from where will*
> *my help come?*

Psalm 121:1

April 4   Answers

W hen I was a wise-youngster I anticipated that by the time I reached my present age I would know the answers to the important questions of life.

Now I am a wise-oldster. I do not have the answers as I expected; moreover, I no longer ask the questions. Instead, I am now immersed in profound awe and rapt respect for mystery:

the mystery of life;

the mystery of God;

the mystery of love;

the mystery of me;

the mystery of the question.

> *What does the* LORD *require of you but to do*
> *justice, and to love kindness, and to walk*
> *humbly with your God?*

Micah 6:8

April 5   Blooming

B loom where you are planted." That popular saying sounds so simple and natural.

But, I wonder, did the author recall the parable of the

73

sower who scattered seed over a variety of terrains —not all of them hospitable to a plant? Many of those seeds never survived to the blooming stage.

Whether we are seeds or bulbs, whether we are carefully planted or scattered carelessly, taking root and growing and blooming is far from easy. Much of life seems neither nurturing nor kind to cultivating plants or people.

If I'm to bloom, however, I'd like to envision myself as a bulb-flower, perhaps a tulip or crocus or daffodil—or even my favorite, an amaryllis. But considering all the confusion and searching in my life, I think I was planted upside down!

> *Listen to me, my faithful children, and blossom like a rose growing by a stream of water. Send out fragrance like incense, and put forth blossoms like a lily. Scatter the fragrance, and sing a hymn of praise; bless the Lord for all his works.*
>
> **Sirach 39:13-14**

April 6   Share

We often encourage the young to share their toys and books, candy and cookies.

It is often harder for children—and, for that matter, adults—to learn to share disappointments and victories, tears of joy and sorrow, defeats and doubts and dreams.

But when the inner self is shared, what is of the outside is shared easily and generously.

> *When she has found it, she calls together her friends and neighbors, saying, "Rejoice with me, for I have found the coin that I had lost."*
>
> **Luke 15:9**

April 7   Courage

As my friend Barb observed, "It takes courage to grow old." No debate about that statement!

There is, of course, the specter of death that prods our courage. But often the greatest courage is needed to face what may precede that time of ultimate transition: pain, loss of independence, mental confusion, loss of sight or mobility, loneliness, loss of dignity, helplessness, outliving friends and family. Defying these possibilities requires courage of heroic proportions.

After all the years of teaching-by-example our kids and grandkids, the greatest challenge is left for the last.

Growing old is not for wimps.

> *I walk before the LORD in the land of the living.*
> **Psalm 116:9**

April 8   Change

Change is integral to life.

In our sorrow, pain, doubt, anxiety, we are consoled by this truth; it is a source of our hope.

In our rejoicing, ecstacy, moments of fulfillment, we are haunted and distracted by this thought; it diminishes our bliss.

For constancy we must look outside the events and people of our existence and focus on God, who is the only true constant in our life.

> *The LORD our God be with us, as he was with our ancestors; may he not leave us or abandon us, but incline our hearts to him, to walk in all his ways, and to keep his commandments, his statutes, and his ordinances, which he commanded our ancestors.*
> **1 Kings 8:57-58**

April 9 — Adoption

Some people adopt because of a personal need for fulfillment. Others adopt to fulfill the needs of the child.

The result is the same—a child who belongs to a whole family, a child who deserves some grand grandparenting.

Whoever welcomes one such child in my name welcomes me.

Matthew 18:5

April 10 — The Church

The two grandmothers greeted each other enthusiastically. One was most eager to talk about the serious problems she had with a teenage grandson and the devastating effect the ordeal was having on the entire family.

"Where is the Church when we need it?" she demanded. "What help is it offering to us—to me and my family—while we are in this domestic hell?"

The other woman responded calmly, "*I* am here—and *I* am the Church!"

An edifice can define a place; a past can preserve traditions; but the Church exists only where people live and proclaim the gospel.

WE are the Church!

Now there are varieties of gifts, but the same Spirit; and there are varieties of services, but the same Lord; and there are varieties of activities, but it is the same God who activates all of them in everyone. To each is given the manifestation of the Spirit for the common good.

1 Corinthians 12:4-7

April 11   Cooking for One

All those years of cooking family meals, of trying to provide enough food to fill hungry kids, hollow-legged teens, and working young adults were poor preparation for this way of life.

Now leftovers last forever; molds proliferate in the refrigerator; a ham defines eternity; the economy size perversely results in waste. I don't even have the right-sized cooking utensils.

Do I want to learn to cook for one?

O God, my God, hear me also—a widow.
Judith 9:4

April 12   The Encounter

The other day I happened to run into Marlys, whom I hadn't seen in many years.

After that humorous ritual of ascertaining that we really did know each other, I inquired most sincerely, "How are you, Marlys?"

"I am, as you can see," she answered, "fat and wrinkled."

Did my face reflect my dismay at such a reply? Was that all Marlys could say about her life? Is "fat and wrinkled" an adequate synopsis of years of living? Did her answer accurately reflect her values, her priorities?

Aren't we grandmothers more than our *packaging*?

To be fat and wrinkled may be time's toll as well as wisdom's attire.

How attractive is wisdom in the aged, and understanding and counsel in the venerable!

Sirach 25:5

April 13 Eating

After spending a week here, one of my grandsons returned home only to hear his mother claim he had gained ten pounds!

I admit that we grandmothers have this "thing" about eating: We are always trying to stuff our grandkids with food. Deep down, we know that all problems cannot be solved by eating; we even recognize that overeating is itself a problem. However, there is something buried inside us that says that food is like hugs and love—we can never have too much.

Perhaps it is part of our genetic memory; the cells of our body remember our ancestral experiences of suffering famine and hunger, of crop failure and unattainable game, of siege and war and poverty. These things we do not readily forget. And so we say "Eat!" and "Want another helping?" and "Ready for dessert?"

We know that not every challenge can be overcome with another piece of chicken or one more chocolate chip cookie. We also know that when hunger is present, life cannot be lived to its fullest.

You prepare a table before me
in the presence of my enemies;
you anoint my head with oil;
my cup overflows.
Surely goodness and mercy shall follow me
all the days of my life,
and I shall dwell in the house of the LORD
my whole life long.

Psalm 23:5-6

April 14   Where Love Begins

The commandment to love others as we love ourselves is based upon an important foundation. That commandment assumes that we love ourselves.

Yet how many of us neither love nor accept ourselves. We have been taught that self-love is wrong; we have been misled into thinking that self-love and self-centeredness are identical.

We have gotten ourselves into theological tangles by confusing self-love with sinful pride or narcissism or egotism; we have been talked into believing that we have a basically depraved human nature. How contrary all that is to the belief that we are made in the image and likeness of God.

That commandment to love others as we love ourselves recognizes that only if we do love ourselves are we capable of loving others.

I have loved you with an everlasting love.
Jeremiah 31:3

April 15   Family

A family is a group of people who share secret humor and stories.

There are jokes that defy explanation to outsiders. There are words and looks and actions that have no meaning to those beyond the family bonds. There are common experiences, the very mention of which brings smiles, open laughter, or visible tears to all who are in the family.

Even though related individuals may dwell in a common abode, without shared humor and stories there is no family.

I have said these things to you so that my joy
may be in you, and that your joy may be com-
plete.

John 15:11

April 16   Gift-Givers

We grandmas enjoy giving—especially to our grandkids. If we are on a tight budget we somehow find the money for grandchild-directed items; and even when we're extra busy we still find opportunities to make gifts.

Although gift-giving can be abused, we grandmas know that the well chosen gift can be an effective communication. It can address the individuality of *this* grandchild; it can broaden interests; it can convey love and affirmation; it can be an example of generosity and selflessness; it can even convey love and affirmation of the grandchild's parents.

The wisely chosen, lovingly given gift can indeed be a manifestation of God's love for us all.

> *(Tabitha) was devoted to good works and acts of*
> *charity.*

Acts 9:36

April 17   Going to Town

Going to town" with my Nonna was an event.
It was a white-gloves-and-hat affair, a time for our best dresses and best manners.
The streetcar ride to town was followed with lunch at the tea

shoppe, a place of privilege for a young girl accompanying her grandmother. It had such an air of refinement and elegant gentility.

Today a child's going to town with Grandma remains an event. But it may mean driving to the shopping mall and eating at a much advertised fast food place.

On occasion, however, it's good to choose someplace different for lunch: a place of privilege for a youngster accompanying Grandmother, a place of refinement and elegant gentility.

Some things are difficult to improve.

> *Let your gentleness be known to everyone.*
> **Philippians 4:5**

April 18   Home Blessing

O Divine Source of All Blessings,
> bless this home!
> Make of it a place of joy and peace,
of health and wholeness,
of restful sleep,
of good eating and abundance,
of beauty and music and dance,
of courage and compassion,
of acceptance,
of forgiveness and gratitude and hospitality,
of growth and learning and wisdom,
of stories and parables and visions and prayers.
Make of it a place of love.
Amen.

> *The place on which you are standing is holy ground.*
>
> **Exodus 3:5**

April 19   The Sound of Music

Movies about beauty—the inner beauty of people, the beauty of God's creation, the beauty of music, the beauty of the love between a man and a woman?

Movies about commitment?

Movies about families and kids, filled with laughter and love?

Movies about people who truly care for one another?

Movies about people who willingly sacrifice the material things of life for what is of lasting value?

Movies about the importance of faith in God, faith in humanity?

Does anyone make such movies anymore?

When the grandkids visit and we run out of things to do—or are tired from all the things we've done—I dig through the videos. "Hey kids, let's watch *The Sound of Music!*"

> *Bless the God of all, who everywhere works*
> *great wonders, who fosters our growth from*
> *birth, and deals with us according to his mercy.*
> *May he give us gladness of heart, and may there*
> *be peace in our days.*

Sirach 50:22-23

April 20   Handicaps

By the time we've become grandmothers we realize that everyone is handicapped in some way.

All of us encounter people who are more talented than we. There are people who surpass us musically or artistically or athletically; people gifted with scientific or mathematical ability;

people with a flare for languages or dealing with kids; people with a green thumb or a knack for business; people who are self-disciplined or well-organized or quick-witted; people more graceful, more patient, more imaginative or creative than we.

We readily admit that compared to these others we appear challenged or handicapped.

Yet while we customarily describe others by what they can do, what talents they possess, what jobs they perform, what relationships they sustain, that is not how we speak of the so-called "handicapped." Why is it that when we describe them we often bypass their varied talents and focus on their limitations? Why is it that we describe those with "handicaps" by what they can't do?

How I would resent being labeled by *my* handicaps!

In his own image God made humankind.

Genesis 9:6

April 21   "I Love You!"

I Love You!"
Words never said too often to
spouse,

     parents,

         children,

            grandchildren,

              friends.

Let love be genuine...love one another with mutual affection; outdo one another in showing honor....Contribute to the needs of the saints; extend hospitality to strangers.

Romans 12:9,10,13

April 22 — Joy

Sometimes joy seems far from me. There are too many concerns and worries, too many insecurities, decisions, disagreements.

It is at times like this that I remind myself that the virtue of joy does not exist only in the absence of problems. In such happy instances there is nothing special about joy's presence. But it is precisely the fact that joy can exist in the midst of concerns and worries and insecurities that makes it a virtue.

Joy is that core deep within us of the Holy Spirit that assures us we are ever in the love and mercy of God. The virtue of joy is the healing and strengthening power that comes from this awareness of God's presence. Joy has creative, restoring properties to renew us when we feel overwhelmed with concerns; joy stimulates us to begin again, our burdens lightened by our knowledge that God is ever with and within us.

Rejoice always.
1 Thessalonians 5:16

April 23 — Model of God

The idea that *I* am a child's model of God is a scary thought. Yet I know very well that for children, all adults serve as models for God. We are God's "stand-ins" on earth. And while Mom and Dad are certainly regarded by their children as authority figures, we who are the parents-of-a-parent may be regarded with added awe.

That thought fills me with awe, along with alarm and humility and determination and trepidation.

> *Can a woman forget her nursing child, or show no compassion for the child of her womb? Even these may forget, yet I will not forget you.*
>
> **Isaiah 49:15**

April 24   Litany of Life

I call upon all the saints of heaven to intercede for us before the throne of God.

All you who knew life, who ran and laughed and prayed and watched amazing sunsets, pray for all those denied the fullness of life.

All you who lived abundantly, who read and sang and dreamed, who praised God fervently and loved with passion, pray for all those denied the fullness of life.

All you who knew fulfillment and suffering and hope, who experienced grief and the comfort of friends, pray for all those denied the fullness of life.

All you whose gift of life was swept away in the womb water, who never knew joy or challenge, who never feared or cried or laughed into tears, pray for all those denied the fullness of life.

> *I call heaven and earth to witness against you today that I have set before you life and death, blessings and curses. Choose life.*
>
> **Deuteronomy 30:19**

April 25   That Age

My grandchild was at *that* age.

As I said to the parents, "I love kids at that age—but I can love them better from afar!"

How long, O LORD?

Isaiah 6:11

April 26   Intimidated

I can stop in anytime, unannounced, at Cynthia's and her place sparkles with nary an item out of place. If I stay for coffee she always has something, made from scratch, fresh out of the oven.

She sews her own clothes, along with the cutest things for her grandkids; she sends handmade birthday and Easter and Christmas cards.

With seeming effortlessness she can host an extended family gathering on the night before she is to leave on a trip.

Cynthia is the first in the neighborhood to take homemade chicken soup to someone ill; she's the one who usually takes up a memorial collection when there's been a death.

Somehow I just know that everything in her freezer is dated and labeled, and I'd guess she probably doesn't own a photograph that is not identified and mounted in an album.

Cynthia is a wonderfully kind and loving person. Why do I feel intimidated?

My child, honor yourself with humility, and give yourself the esteem you deserve.

Sirach 10:28

April 27 — Parable

There are parables in Scripture.
There are parables in songs and nursery rhymes.
There are parables in stories and histories.
There are parables in religions and mythologies.
The greatest parable is life itself.

Life is a parable trying to speak to us.
With all our senses,
Let us listen!

> *Let the wise also hear and gain in learning,*
> *and the discerning acquire skill,*
> *to understand a proverb and a figure,*
> *the words of the wise and their riddles.*

Proverbs 1:5-6

April 28 — Pre-Funeral Eulogies

At my granddaughter's request we were attending the funeral of the grandmother of a close friend.

As I listened to the several eulogies of this woman I had never met, one question kept recurring: Did anyone ever say these kind, affirming words to her while she was alive?

I heard thoughtfulness praised; belief in God exalted; talents eulogized; dedication to family commended; generosity complimented; faithfulness extolled; courage acclaimed; humor admired; selflessness lauded.

But, I wondered, did anyone ever say any of these things to the living person?

> *Therefore encourage one another and build up each other.*

1 Thessalonians 5:11

April 29   They Remember

The most joyful and the most sorrowful utterances,
The most consoling and the most disheartening
         comments,
All begin with the identical words:
"I remember what you said to me...."

Kids do remember.

They remember us at our best and at our worst;

They remember our words, both our finest and our most shameful.

They remember!

> *A gentle tongue is a tree of life,*
> *but perverseness in it breaks the spirit.*

Proverbs 15:4

April 30   Trivial?

Some things in life are trivial and should be regarded as such. However, that is not true of our own life experiences. There is validity in what we each see and do and learn and experience, for God speaks to us through our life's happenings. To think about our life, to evaluate our growth—these are valuable activities and worth communicating to our grandchildren.

As a friend of mine is fond of saying, "It is the devil who teaches us to trivialize our own experiences."

> *Jesus, full of the Holy Spirit, returned from the Jordan and was led by the Spirit in the wilderness, where for forty days he was tempted by the devil....Jesus answered (the devil),"It is written, 'Worship the LORD your God, and serve only him.'"*

Luke 4:1-2,8

May 1 — Affirmation Party

My neighbor Sally gave an affirmation party. Her goal was to create an environment that would encourage family members to say the loving and supportive thoughts so often never verbalized.

All her kids and grandkids, instead of bringing the usual potluck contributions, brought one or more positive statements about each family member.

It was a time of embarrassment, shyness, hesitation; it was a time of enthusiasm and skepticism. But it was also a time filled with many, many surprises.

"I never thought you ever noticed that!"

"Why didn't you tell me?"

"I'm amazed that you remember my doing that!"

"I didn't realize you cared so much!"

The party wasn't perfect, since the party-goers weren't perfect. But it was good—very, very good.

> *How sweet are your words to my taste,*
> *sweeter than honey to my mouth!*
> **Psalm 119:103**

May 2 — Her-Stories

Full recognition of mothers and nurturers extends beyond the giving of flowers and candy and sentimental greeting cards. Such recognition will not be attained until *her-stories* are as well known as *his-stories*.

Textbooks are full of *his-stories*, of wars and governments and explorations and conquests.

Missing from these texts are *her-stories*, the narratives of the women whose names *his-story* considers unimportant—women known only as daughters of men, sisters of men, concubines and mistresses of men, wives of men, mothers of men, widows of men.

Her-stories tell of women and children and survival, of love and family life and culture, of giving birth and nurturing, of keeping faith, of maintaining hope, of persevering through sorrows and pain. *Her-stories* tell of searching for God in life's dailiness, of finding God everywhere, of the astounding discovery of the love affair that God has with each of us.

Mother's Day calls us to focus on all the *her-stories* of life!

> *All ate and were filled; and they took up what was left over of the broken pieces, twelve baskets full. And those who ate were about five thousand men, besides women and children.*

Matthew 14:20-21

May 3   Appreciation

Over the years my friend Helen has introduced me to a different facet of the virtue of appreciation. Through Helen I have learned that we can express our admiration for objects of beauty and creativity and talent, not only by acquiring and possessing them, but also by passing them on to others.

Helen has been known to give others gifts which she has received. They are not to be considered as hand-me-downs, however, for during their passage through various owners they have become twice-blessed—or multi-blessed—gifts. These items, having been gratefully received by Helen and enjoyed by her, have thus increased in value.

I recently received a "Thinking of You" note from Helen. The card, crafted by a local artist, was certainly worthy of framing. Helen, in typical fashion, wrote her message on a Post-it rather than the card itself, so I could, if desired, send that card on to another.

Through Helen I have learned that it is not necessary to possess something to indicate our regard for it; we can also show our appreciation by giving it to others.

> *Like good stewards of the manifold grace of God, serve one another with whatever gift each of you has received.*
>
> **1 Peter 4:10**

May 4   Be Nice to Me

The courteous bloodmobile personnel are anxious that we donors are not kept waiting. I fill out the forms, answer the nurse's questions, have my pulse, temperature and blood pressure taken.

Donating blood—often I really don't think about it ahead of my appointment time. But lying there on the cot, while the bag slowly fills with the liquid of life, I become meditative. Who will receive my blood? An automobile accident victim? A child suffering from leukemia? A person with AIDS? Or cancer? A woman who has just given birth? Or a newborn?

It really doesn't matter. As I leave I proudly wear my American Red Cross sticker-badge:

Be nice to me

I gave blood today

✚ **American Red Cross**

> *How does God's love abide in anyone who has the world's goods and sees a brother or sister in need and yet refuses help?*
>
> **1 John 3:17**

May 5 — Grandparent Love

Only a grandparent can love a child in her or his historical wholeness!

The LORD bless you and keep you;
the LORD make his face to shine upon you, and
be gracious to you;
the LORD lift up his countenance upon you,
and give you peace.

Numbers 6:24-26

May 6 — Chaos

Chaos" can describe any of several states of being:
(1) That which existed before God created;
(2) That which exists after parenthood;
(3) That which is necessary in order that children can learn.

We persnickety adults, in our desire for order and neatness, often try to prevent chaos from occurring. Children, however, need chaos to enable them to learn what order is. And, like God, they seem to prefer chaos for their creating.

In the beginning...the earth was a formless void
and darkness covered the face of the deep.

Genesis 1:1-2

I remember those early class reunions, when our discussions centered on lifetime plans, bright beginnings, hopeful starts. How apparent was our need to impress one another.

With the passage of years, the stories of unmitigated progress became interspersed with those of restarts and postponed beginnings, of temporary losses and direction changes as we continued to jockey for position in the unofficial "class standings."

Then the bragging of accomplishments began to give way to the humble uttering of personal tragedies and heartache, the painful narration of insights gained through inestimable mistakes, the revelation of dreams abandoned, the confession of wealth lost.

As time progressed the boasting of personal triumphs was often replaced with hope-filled tales of offspring, of graphic accounts of illnesses and operations, and of remembrances of classmates and others already gone to eternal rest.

As the reunions continue today the emphasis has gradually focused upon our common bond of survival. It took a lifetime of living for us to realize it is our humanity that unites us all—not the school we happened to attend.

> **Be kind to one another, tenderhearted, forgiving**
> **one another, as God in Christ has forgiven you.**
> **Ephesians 4:32**

There is a mistaken belief that love is blind. The truth is that *infatuation* is blind; pride and self-centeredness distort vision; ambition blurs; and lack of faith can bring on early darkness. But love itself sees clearly and penetratingly.

Love sees not only the "now" but also the "may be." It looks beyond current limitations to the promises of future fulfillment and eternal perfection. This clear-sighted vision gives love the potential power to awaken the forces within the one loved.

All of us need someone who looks at us with the perceptive vision of love and recognizes our latent good; someone to see those wonderful qualities which we ourselves do not recognize; someone to uncover our embryonic virtues and buried seeds of talent; someone to unleash the dreams yet undreamed, music not yet composed, poetry waiting to be sung. Love sees the hidden treasures of intellect and imagination and creativity; love sees love, not yet flamed, awaiting a human spark to ignite it.

Grandparent love has the vision to see the entirety of each grandchild's being and still say, "God did indeed create well!"

> *"What no eye has seen, nor ear heard, nor the human heart conceived, what God has prepared for those who love him"—these things God has revealed to us through the Spirit.*
>
> **1 Corinthians 2:9-10**

May 9   The Divine Smile

The censure of nearby worshipers was obvious: We were a distraction.

We were at my grandson's grade school graduation liturgy and everyone in our family was laughing. To us, everything seemed funny—although the people sitting around us saw very little humor. But then, they hadn't been part of this family for this fumbling, bumbling, Marx Brothers kind of day. By dinnertime we had progressed to the state where we had our choice of either being at each other's throats or laughing together. Fortunately, our frazzled nerves translated everything into humor and our family was engaged in giggles and stage whispers and private jokes that could only be explained with, "You had to be there."

As the disapproving looks continued I thought of Christ with his "family." Together they endured the pressures of travel and crowds and preaching. They dealt with those ever-present elements of humanity: Peter's impetuosity; John's youth; Jesus' weariness; the Pharasees' surveillance. Surely they too had at times experienced "one of those days" and laughed about it.

And I was confident that God understood our seeming lack of reverence and was smiling with us.

> **A joyful heart is life itself,
> and rejoicing lengthens one's life span.**
>
> Sirach 30:22

May 10   Enjoy!

Today, God,
     I resolve to enjoy life!

I do not wait for all my problems to be solved—I enjoy this minute.

I do not wait for all my wants to be met—I enjoy this space in the universe.

I do not wait for all my dreams to become reality—I enjoy this place in time.

I do not wait until those around me are perfect—I enjoy them in the wholeness of their being.

I do not wait until I attain perfection—I enjoy myself in the totality of my being.

I do not wait until I am in heaven—I enjoy your divine presence within and around me.

    Today, now—I enjoy life!

> **Live as children of light.**
>
> Ephesians 5:8

My friends proudly showed me their fiftieth anniversary scrapbook. Mounted in the book, along with the congratulatory cards and letters, were many small slips of paper—so many that they filled several album pages.

Each paper began "I remember when...." followed by a family member's description of a memory of the anniversary couple. While most of the memories were happy or humorous or comforting, others were sad or haunting or bittersweet, covering the spectrum of family life.

The anniversary couple told of an entire afternoon spent with the family opening the small envelopes containing the "memories." Everyone laughed and wept and hugged and gloried in all those remembrances.

Looking again at the album, I realized it was more than a scrapbook. This collection of stories of events and people and love—both human and divine—was truly a "family bible." That book, entitled with their name, was one more addition to the story of salvation history—the story of which we all are part.

> *The days of a good life are numbered,*
> *but a good name lasts forever.*

Sirach 41:13

Green is my favorite color. Although I don't have much green in my wardrobe or decor, I like green because it is the dominant color of things that grow.

How I love to watch the leafing-out of trees and bushes as the small, delicate buds gradually become transformed into the full rich green of abundant life. I enjoy fields of growing things and seeing green interspersed with the multihued flowers and produce. How relaxing and restoring are areas of grass—lawns and golf courses and sod farms. And, of course, there's the green of Christmas trees and all evergreens and of our year-round companion houseplants.

Green is the color of hope; it is the liturgical color for ordinary time—that time apart from the major feasts and seasons in the Christian calendar.

Green speaks of the vitality of life. It speaks courageously and enthusiastically of belief in love and spring's life after winter's death.

Green is my favorite color.

> *Let the heavens be glad, and let the earth rejoice;*
> *let the sea roar, and all that fills it;*
> *let the field exult, and everything in it.*
> *Then shall all the trees of the forest sing for joy*
> *before the Lord.*

Psalm 96:11-13

May 13   Graduation

When I graduated, many years ago, I recall the parents of the graduates being asked to stand for recognition. That was followed by, "Will the grandparents of the graduates please stand."

Now at graduations a different request could be made, "Will the graduates who are grandparents please stand."

There is no age limit on learning.

> *Give instruction to the wise,*
> *and they will become wiser still;*
> *teach the righteous*
> *and they will gain in learning.*

Proverbs 9:9

May 14   Bowing to the Absurd

I'm convinced that there are moments when the only term that adequately describes life is *absurd*.

Absurdity is not what we planned or what we expected; the unpredictability, the harshness, the injustice of life—these are neither what we want nor what we believe we deserve.

The only possible survival technique at such times is to bow to the absurd and hand over the frustrations, the questions and the doubts to the Divine.

And then we stand tall, with heads courageously held high, and LAUGH!

> **Sarah laughed.**
>
> **Genesis 18:12**

May 15   If You Knew Me...

The newspaper ad pictured a friendly-looking middle-aged man breathing oxygen through tubes and lying in a hospital bed. The caption read "If you knew me, you'd help me."

The ad included the usual stats about the man: his age and education and job, his wife's name, the number of years of their marriage, the fact that they had three children...and three weddings scheduled on the family calendar. Below the picture were descriptions of him by friends: a man of faith, of commitment to family and community, a man valued as a friend. However, this man's life was dependent upon an organ donation, for without this transplant soon he would die.

What a powerful, vivid reminder to us. Whenever we are whirling in the trauma of the loss of someone close to us, it is difficult to think of others. Yet that is precisely when we must remember that the lives of people like the man in the ad are dependent upon the decisions that we, the survivors, make at that difficult time.

What better memorial could there possibly be than the realization that someone else lives because of a donation from our loved one and our own thoughtfulness?

We walk by faith, not by sight.

2 Corinthians 5:7

May 16   Justice

I t really doesn't matter why we jump into the fight for equality. Eventually we come to the same conclusion: We must recognize the dignity and worth of all peoples.

Perhaps we first come face-to-face with prejudice as a female, a *mujerista*, an African American, an Asian, a single parent, a lesbian, a person in a wheelchair or the grandmother of a person with AIDS. Then we begin battling the barriers and roadblocks that have been erected before us by our society, our Church, our communities, our school, our neighbors or even our own families.

It really doesn't matter why we jump into the fight for equality. Eventually we come to the same conclusion: We must use our own talents and abilities to reshape the world into a place where there are no barriers.

There is one body and one Spirit, just as you
were called to be the one hope of your calling,
one LORD, one faith, one baptism, one God and
Father of all, who is above all and through all
and in all.

Ephesians 4:4-6

Everyone's moving! Moving from homes into apartments; from condos into retirement facilities; from apartments to assisted-living complexes; from independent quarters to shared living spaces with kids and grandkids; from retirement buildings to nursing homes.

Never before have there been so many of us grandparents; never before have so many of us been on the move.

And never before have so many of us been forced to move, to adapt, to learn new ways, to begin again.

Isn't there an age limit on having to begin yet one more time?

> **The LORD *went in front of them in a pillar of cloud by day, to lead them along the way, and in a pillar of fire by night, to give them light, so that they might travel by day and by night.***
>
> **Exodus 13:21**

Some of us grandmothers are LDGs, otherwise known as Long Distance Grandmas. We LDGs are readily identifiable by our extensive and handy stock of mailing and shipping supplies. To put into these containers we have assorted incidentals, determined by our grandchildren's ages:

pictures;

puzzles;

magazine articles;

newspaper cartoons;

inspirational stories;

books;

freebies from fairs and open houses;

cookies, candy, airline peanuts;

coupons from the fast-food chains;

money in various denominations;

and, of course, stacks of cards for every

occasion.

> *For the promise is for you, for your children,*
> *and for all who are far away, everyone whom*
> *the Lord our God calls to him.*

Acts 2:39

May 19   Pregnancy

E very time I see a pregnant woman I am flooded with emotions:

Awe in the presence of creation;

Reassurance in witnessing this statement of belief that humanity
has a future;

Remembrances of both the death-defying pain and the ecstatic satisfaction of giving birth;

Joy in the presence of new life;

Concern for the future of this child;

Desire to pray for the family;

Feelings of responsibility for the world to be inhabited by the child;

And overwhelming gratitude that the pregnant woman isn't me!

> *The fruit of the womb (is) a reward.*

Psalm 127:3

I dreamed of a young girl—she was my great-great-grand-daughter. I can't explain just how I knew that, but, in that way-of-knowing in dreams, I knew.

"The scene was a garbage dump. She was standing there all alone, surrounded by mountains of debris extending as far as I could see. For some reason, each mound—and they were gigantic—consisted of identical items, as if someone had very carefully sorted every item of garbage.

"Even though I was far enough away to take in the entire scene, I was able to identify the items of each debris-mound. One mound consisted only of plastic spoons, another of forks, another of knives; there was a tremendous pile of those little plastic sample bottles, another of individual ketchup packets; there were mountains of various items we today call 'disposable' or 'one-time-use.'

"My great-great-granddaughter never said one word in this dream. But she walked slowly between the garbage heaps, shaking her head sadly."

> *For how can I bear to see the calamity that is*
> *coming on my people? Or how can I bear to see*
> *the destruction of my kindred?*
>
> **Esther 8:6**

Parent is the only vocational title that we carry with us throughout our life; we never retire from that job.

Our children, grandchildren, family will be our only

worldly assets with us in eternity.

> *Your kingdom come. Your will be done, on earth as it is in heaven.*

Matthew 6:10

May 22   Who Decides?

Who do we let define parental success?

The dentist who intimates parental neglect because of a kid's cavity?

The Madison Avenue detergent ad writer who declares success is measured by the cleanliness of kids' clothes?

The school principal who remembers only the names of room parents?

The sales clerk who hints at social alienation if our young do not wear clothes with the *in* logo?

The church's youth minister who records all who attend the outings?

Other parents who measure success in terms of games (or performances or practices or recitals) attended?

Neighbors who arbitrarily determine the proper age for the young to marry or to attend college or to become parents or...?

Who do we let define our success as a parent?

> *I am the light of the world. Whoever follows me will never walk in darkness but will have the light of life.*

John 8:12

The word "worry" has an Anglo-Saxon origin and means to strangle or choke or twist.

Sometimes when we want to break a piece of wire we *worry* it, twisting it around and around until it breaks.

By our *worry* we can strangle, choke, or twist to the breaking point those around us.

Worry is a powerfully effective, but devious, technique of control.

> ***Do not worry about anything, but in everything***
> ***by prayer and supplication with thanksgiving let***
> ***your requests be made known to God.***
>
> **Philippians 4:6**

May 24   Acceptance

The rejection of a child can be very subtle; it can be as simple as the lack of complete acceptance.

The happy domestic mom surrounded by her hand-loomed rugs has a daughter whose passion is drag racing. The father who has known the batting averages of all the major leaguers since he was eight years old has a kid who prefers acting to sports. The musician has a kid who's tone-deaf. The *macho* dad has a son who is gay. The dainty female finds herself grandma to a bunch of noisy, raucous boys.

To accept a child is to recognize that all children are gifts from a loving God. They come to us wrapped in surprises. The acceptance of every child is an act of faith in God, faith in the child, and faith in ourselves as we parent or grandparent.

Acceptance is our first task; it is also one of the most demanding and often repeated tasks. However, acceptance is also one of the most rewarding of tasks, for it allows us to recognize and empower each child to fulfill whatever potentials God has placed within that particular and continuously developing gift to the world.

> *Those who are wise understand these things;*
> *those who are discerning know them. For the*
> *ways of the LORD are right, and the upright*
> *walk in them, but transgressors stumble in them.*
>
> **Hosea 14:9**

May 25   The Sale

The proceedings had begun early. At noon I brought lunch to the young adults conducting their parents' estate sale. This painful dismantling of their childhood home continued the grieving process of these people I had known all their lives.

I watched them deal arbitrarily with the customers. For the professional garage sale people there was no lowering of prices; for neighbors it was "Could you use that? Please take it. Mom would love for you to have it." And when residents of the nearby home for the mentally handicapped showed interest in Dad's hobby equipment, they said, "I think Dad would be pleased if you'd accept that as a remembrance of him."

Exhausting hours later the sale closed and the remnants were gathered for the St. Vincent DePaul Society. The accumulations of two lifetimes had been converted into so little money. But I recalled with a shiver the disposal of a different estate. Those heirs, not bothering with a sale or even a donation to the needy, had a dumpster carry away everything.

"Your parents would approve of what you did," I told my friends.

> *I will turn their mourning into joy, I will com-*
> *fort them, and give them gladness for sorrow.*
>
> **Jeremiah 31:13**

May 26   Simplicity

Affirming others need not be complicated. Often a simple "Wow!" will suffice.

Sing aloud, O daughter Zion; shout, O Israel!
Rejoice and exult with all your heart, O daughter Jerusalem!

Zephaniah 3:14

May 27   Special Child

Using the term "special child" to describe an individual with a handicap is common. It is not wise, however, for in so doing we may lose sight of the uniqueness of each and every child.

The other danger inherent in the term is that we may think of these children as being in a category separated from the rest of us. We may thereby deprive them of their God-given innate humanity. Children with handicaps are not angels; neither are they the embodiment of God's curse. They are human beings who, no matter what the handicap, are much more *like* us than they are *different* from us.

These kids—and adults—have the same basic needs as the rest of us. They need food, clothing, shelter, medical care, education. Also, like all of us, they need to be loved and to love; to be recognized as individuals; to be part of the community; to develop a relationship with God.

We are all more alike than we are different.

*There is no longer Jew or Greek, there is no
longer slave or free, there is no longer male and
female; for all of you are one in Christ Jesus.*

Galatians 3:28

May 28   There's God

A woman, in much mental distress, approached the Wise
Man. "Sir," she said, "I fear that I do not love God."
The Wise Man asked, "Is there no one that you love?"
"I deeply love my grandchildren," was her answer.

"Then there, in your love and duty to those children, is your love
and duty to God."

> *Truly I tell you, just as you did it to one of the
> least of these who are members of my family,
> you did it to me.*

Matthew 25:40

May 29   Prayer in the Wake of Violence

O crucified-and-risen Lord,
when you walked upon this earth
you tasted violence;
though innocent,
you suffered as the guilty.

We ask that you,
the Prince of Peace,
cleanse this place of its memories of violence.
Wipe away its echo-cries of hatred and pain

and leave only laughter and love.
Transform this place,
this neighborhood,
this world,
as you transformed the cross—
into a symbol of love
and of peace. Amen.

> *Blessed are the peacemakers, for they will be*
> *called children of God.*

Matthew 5:9

May 30   Our Story

My grandkid's class visited Washington. While it's a wonderful opportunity for them, I know that D.C. hoards its wealth for those of us rich in years. This is *our* city, for its importance lies in our importance, in who we are, in what we have done and what we continue to do. D.C. is a narration of achievements, a reliving of emotions; but most of all, it is a city that helps form us and that we help form.

Exhibited in the Smithsonian is our story—displays of our ethnic heritage, our trades and labor unions, our religions and organizations, our crafts and music and art, our science and engineering. The government halls echo with the speeches of Americans whose words we remember when they were first uttered. We know the Lincoln Memorial as not just a memorial to a dead president, but also as the site of Martin Luther King's "I Have a Dream" speech. Here, in the midst of larger-than-life monuments, we can trace with our fingers the names of the casualties of the Vietnam War—a war in *our* lifetime—and reaffirm *our* commitment to recognizing the importance of each individual.

It's great for the young to visit D.C., but it takes the bonus of years to appreciate it fully.

> *All the ends of the earth*
> *shall remember and turn to the LORD;*
> *and all the families of the nations*
> *shall worship before him.*
> *For dominion belongs to the LORD,*
> *and he rules over the nations.*

Psalm 22:27-28

May 31   "Surprise! I'm Pregnant!"

No pregnancy is ever *convenient*; nor is any pregnancy ever quite according to plan.

Consider that memorable visit of Mary and Elizabeth. There is Mary, young, confused, not yet married, worried about Joseph's reaction to the incredible news of her pregnancy. Could he possibly accept her fantastic story?

And then there's Elizabeth, coping with a pregnancy in her advanced age, along with a husband suddenly struck speechless. What was going on in the world?

Two pregnant women. Today many in our society would encourage such women to have abortions, for Mary was too young for motherhood and Elizabeth too old.

Yet amidst the confusion and weariness, what faith these women exhibited! Would that every pregnancy could be greeted with such joy.

> *When Elizabeth heard Mary's greeting, the child*
> *leaped in her womb. And Elizabeth was filled*
> *with the Holy Spirit and exclaimed with a loud*
> *cry, "Blessed are you among women, and*
> *blessed is the fruit of your womb."*

Luke 1:41-42

111

June 1   "Ain't Been Done!"

Everyone called her "Nonnie." She was the neighborhood grandma back when our kids were young.

Nonnie had class. From her carefully coiffured silver hair to the tips of her pedicured feet, she was a *somebody*.

The kids loved her and Nonnie returned that love. Nonnie's regard for each individual was always soon reflected in the kids' respect for one another—and for themselves—when they were around her. From Nonnie they learned that it was possible to have fun without losing their dignity or demeaning others. In her presence, the notorious toughies selfcensored their own speech and conduct. But should someone exceed the boundary of propriety, Nonnie would put her head back, look down her nose, and, in a mock-haughty voice, declare, "It just ain't been done!"

Nonnie's "It just ain't been done!" was sufficient to bring an errant kid back into line. Her boundaries, established by kindness and compassion, were effectively enforced—not by confrontation or force, but simply by her young friends' desire for her approval.

How different our society would be if more of us could learn to say—with Nonnie's effectiveness—"It just ain't been done!"

> *She opens her mouth with wisdom,*
> *and the teaching of kindness is on her tongue.*
>
> **Proverbs 31:26**

June 2   "Batter Up!"

STRIKE!"

"You blind? That was a ball!"

"Ya gotta be kiddin! That was a strike if ever I saw one!"

"Will you two quit fighting and get on with the game!"

Having a baseball game nearby is tolerable; having constant arguments just outside my window is not. The kids can't agree on boundaries, rules, calls, bases, or even who is on which team.

Kids in formal recreation programs play by rules. However, organized sports cannot teach them appreciation for those rules. Time-consuming sandlot arguing is the only way for young people to realize the need for regulations. It helps the kids understand that rules exist not to frustrate but to free participants to play and enjoy a game.

All of us have rules and laws—of family, of society, and of God—that we are expected to obey. With experience we eventually realize that the commandments of God exist not to frustrate but to free all of us to live and enjoy life to the fullest.

> *Happy are those who fear the LORD,*
> *who greatly delight in his commandments.*

Psalm 112:1

June 3 Brats!

Not all kids are angels.
Not all kids are fun to be with or delightful to entertain.
Not all kids are polite and well-behaved.
Not all kids are obedient and considerate.
Not all kids are appreciative and receptive.
Not all kids are especially likeable.
There are some kids who deserve the appellation *brats*.
But even these kids have grandmothers.
And it is our job to love them.

> *A wise child loves discipline,*
> *but a scoffer does not listen to rebuke.*

Proverbs 13.1

I watched my son reading to his daughter.

This was not a typical "kid-on-Dad's-lap" scene. Dad was leaning back in the lounge chair with his newborn babe, somewhat resembling a friendly parasite, lying contentedly on his chest. She lay there peacefully, lullabied with the soothing sound of her father's voice as he read aloud the newspaper editorials.

My son had learned from his dad that it's never too early to start reading to his daughter; it's never too early to begin the bonding that lasts two lifetimes; it's never too early to begin the process of being Dad.

> *(The LORD) shielded him, cared for him, guard-*
> *ed him as the apple of his eye. As an eagle stirs*
> *up its nest, and hovers over its young; as it*
> *spreads its wings, takes them up, and bears them*
> *aloft on its pinions, the LORD alone guided him.*
>
> **Deuteronomy 32:10-12**

When I was young, we were rewarded and praised for conformity and uniformity. We were told *exactly* how to do things; and, of course, we were to stay inside the lines when we colored.

But now that I'm a grandma how I value individuality and creativity. Not only is it exciting to see such qualities in my grandchildren, but I've come to recognize and celebrate these facets of God. God is the first and supreme artist, with creation the unsurpassable artistic endeavor.

God has gifted us human beings with that same creativity, for the image of God within us is that creative potential. It is our heritage, as human beings, to be creative. The Holy Spirit, the Dove of Creativity, sparks our imagination and vision and inventiveness.

How I encourage, celebrate, affirm, rejoice in the creativity within us all!

Do not quench the Spirit.
1 Thessalonians 5:19

June 6 Charity

When I was young and heard the term "Christian charity," I envisioned great deeds and extreme self-denial. I thought of Damien ministering to the lepers or missionaries traveling into headhunter territories. I certainly never thought of parents ministering within the family. But now, having survived many years of motherhood and graduated into grandmotherhood, I've come to reassess the call to holiness and Christian charity that we all have. That call to love one another, which comes, for most of us, in the context of daily family life, does indeed include great deeds and extreme self-denial.

No novice mistress is more demanding than a perpetual-motion toddler. The cloister's repetitive call to prayer is no less restricting than the responsibility for a family's three daily meals, year after year. At times, the vow of poverty seems appealing when we're faced with a family's financial crises. Just because the people to whom we are ministering are family does not lessen the value of our ministering. And the fact that we may happen to be related to the ones we're trying to convert (who may even at times exhibit somewhat savage traits) mean it is not missionary activity.

Where else does charity begin but in the home?

The commandment we have from him is this:
those who love God must love their brothers and
sisters also.

1 John 4:21

June 7   The Comedian

She came on stage in a *faux-glamorous* outfit featuring a feather boa and a superabundance of bangles. The comedian was a bi-focalled, overly made-up matron in support shoes.

And what was the material for her stand-up comedy act? The crazy, ironic, daily life of today's older woman. The woman that society, family, and doctors readily dismiss; the woman who is at times at the mercy of hormonal roller coasters; the woman replaced by the "trophy" wife; the woman invisible to upscale climbers; the crone living in a youth-worshiping culture.

We laughed—how deeply and wholeheartedly we older women laughed. And then, refreshed and renewed and reaffirmed, we returned to continue our fight to change the world.

Yes, you are our glory and joy!
1 Thessalonians 2:20

June 8   Disposable Kids

A friend once suggested, "God should have given us parents a cardboard-and-plastic child to practice on before sending us the real thing. Then we could try out our child-raising theories on this disposable model instead of the flesh-and-blood reality. After we have made all our mistakes we could toss aside the make-believe kid and get started on the real one. Or...we just might reconsider the whole vocation!"

Like that mother, I too would have preferred practicing my motherhood on something less fragile than a human being. Unfortunately, no such experimental model is available. While we have disposable diapers, bottles, thermometers, bibs, tableware, and toys, we don't have disposable kids.

However, even if such a thing were possible I know that it

wouldn't work. Each child is unique; we parents change; times and situations never remain static; the method of child-raising that works for one child may be devastating to another; and that bond that exists between adult and child—that wonderful, frustrating, demanding tie of love—could not be replicated with a disposable model. And so we practice motherhood on the infinitely valuable child entrusted to us, hoping and praying that we don't fail in our task.

> *Do not, therefore, abandon that confidence of*
> *yours; it brings a great reward.*
>
> **Hebrews 10:35**

June 9   "YA-HOO!"

The commuter flight passengers were a civilian army of uniformed business people, armed with *Wall Street Journals* and briefcases. Boarding with this troop—and looking like obvious misfits—were a college student and her younger brother. As the plane taxied down the runway, the older passengers remained indifferent to the maneuver while the youths watched intently as the scene sped by with increasing rapidity. At the moment of liftoff the young boy raised his arms in exhilaration: "YA-HOO!"

The sudden smiles and laughter throughout the plane were proof that the other passengers, through the enthusiasm of a child, were made aware of the moment's magic. Enthusiasm is contagious—we "catch" it from all those around us, but especially from children. By their very existence they remind us of the wonderful gift of life. Kids teach us the magic of silly songs sung out of an inner happiness. They teach us the simplicity of playing with dust particles in a sunbeam, the fun of puddles after a rain, the mystery of watching a potted seed grow. Enthusiasm can work miracles. It can transform duties into acts of love, routine into adventure, and the science of aeronautics into a "YA-HOO!"

> *The prophet Miriam...took a tambourine in her*
> *hand; and all the women went out after her with*
> *tambourines and with dancing. And Miriam*
> *sang to them: "Sing to the LORD...."*

Exodus 15:20

June 10   Family Justice

Family justice is not the blind justice of the law which, in the ideal, treats everyone identically. In the family, giving to each child equally may mean that one child has a surplus while another does not have enough.

True family justice is the all-seeing justice of love, which gives sufficiently to each person according to that one's need.

Such justice is a necessary ingredient for family happiness.

> *To do righteousness and justice is more accept-*
> *able to the LORD than sacrifice.*

Proverbs 21:3

June 11   Grace

God's grace lurks everywhere!

It is present at those moments when we are vividly awakened to the unending mysteries of existence and marriage and parenthood.

It is present in the intimacy of passion and quiet, of lovemaking and daily encounter, of communication beyond words.

It is present in the awe-inspiring excitement of birth, the soft touch of the infant feeding at the breast, the smile of a child, the trusting hand-seeking of a youngster, or—wonder-of-wonders—the words of a teenager, "I want your advice."

It is present in the maturity and responsibility of our grown children; it is there in the as the cycle begins again with the birth of our grandchildren.

God's presence, God's grace, God's love are abundantly evident throughout life. Perhaps everything is grace—when we are open to it.

> *See, the home of God is among mortals. He will*
> *dwell with them as their God; they will be his*
> *peoples, and God himself will be with them; he*
> *will wipe every tear from their eyes.*
>
> Revelation 21:3-4

June 12 — Gifts That Burden

I always experience a bit of apprehension when presented with a gift; I guess I've received my share of presents that are burdens in disguise.

I don't mind the gifts that indicate a difference of taste. Perhaps I would not have chosen a particular sweater or pair of earrings or knick-knack—but that's fine. Though these gifts may not be my favorites, I appreciate them deeply, for they speak of the love and thoughtfulness of the givers.

The gifts that make me uncomfortable are the ones that come wrapped in *shoulds*. They focus dramatically at my weak points, my obvious lack of certain talents, or those well-known areas of my life that I consider of lesser importance than does the gift-giver.

I have enough difficulty accepting myself as I am without such finger pointing. Those gifts carry a large price tag, perhaps not for the giver but certainly for the recipient.

> *Rekindle the gift of God that is within you.*
>
> 2 Timothy 1:6

Grandma-Hands

Grandma-hands can be delicate, gentle, graceful hands; or calloused, dirt-stained, strong hands; or long-fingered, agile, skilled hands; or stubby, clumsy, arthritic hands. Grandma-hands can be brown or black or yellow or red or white hands.

No matter what the appearance, our grandma-hands perform many ministries. They soothe, heal, stroke, point, persuade, caress, intercede, warm, beseech, hug, touch, punish, direct, communicate, bless, cool, restrain. Grandma-hands continue the work begun by our Creator-God.

Of the many actions which our grandma-hands perform, the most important is that of reaching out with our hands open. Our hands—and hearts—must be open to receive in the fullness of being in each child, each grandchild. Our hands—and hearts—must be open to release into the fullness of life each child, each grandchild.

Grandma-hands: holy-hands.

> **Let the favor of the LORD our God be upon us,**
> **and prosper for us the work of our hands—**
> **O prosper the work of our hands!**

Psalm 90:17

June 14 Imagination

There was a time when I thought imagination was important only to a few special people, like artists and storytellers and visionaries. But that was before I met people who had no imagination—or else whose imagination had been buried. That's when I began to realize how necessary imagination is to ordinary living.

It takes imagination to envision solutions to problems; if no one envisions solutions, the problems remain. It takes imagination to see that there are alternate ways of achieving goals; otherwise there is no room for diversity. It takes imagination to build; nothing comes into being unless it has first been imagined. It takes imagination to be compassionate; otherwise only what has been personally experienced can evoke emotion. It takes imagination to transfer insights from one area to another; without such crossover learning we do not recognize similarities in relationships, both human and divine.

Without imagination we cannot realize the fullness of our humanity, which is in the image and likeness of God, who created us out of infinite love and unbounded imagination.

> *I can do all things through him who strengthens me.*
>
> **Philippians 4:13**

June 15   Justice and Mercy

O God of Justice and Mercy,
　　Teach us to care!
　For poor kids,
　Teach us, God, to care!
For hungry kids,
　Teach us, God, to care!
For frightened kids,
　Teach us, God, to care!
For lonely kids,
　Teach us, God, to care!
For homeless kids,
　Teach us, God, to care!

For neglected kids,
   Teach us, God, to care!
For all kids everywhere,
   Teach us, God, to care!
      Give justice to the weak and the orphan;
      maintain the right of the lowly and the destitute.
      Rescue the weak and the needy;
      deliver them from the hand of the wicked.

Psalm 82:3-4

June 16   Long Ago

My adult life has been spent
in burying my childhood.

Yet the weight of time is not enough
to keep from reappearing
those memories of long ago.

Though I strain to forget,
the images emerge.
Though I place
a multitude of stones
of loving experiences
upon my childhood cairn,
what happened long ago
yet lives.

   And I say, "O that I had wings like a dove!
      I would fly away and be at rest."

Psalm 55:6

June 17   "Muddling Through"

Kids are always, incontestably, the experts; we adults are just as invariably the inept novices. Our children come to us possessing much knowledge and ability—some of which we would prefer they never acquired. A toddler does not have to be taught how to be a "terrible two"; teenagers know instinctively how to be rebellious. Name any problem that a child can possibly present to adults, and kids know exactly how to present it—and with *panache*!

This childhood conspiracy is amazingly successful in leaving us a minimum of three steps behind our offspring at all times. By the time we have identified the problem, sought information and help, and are on the verge of dealing competently with that problem, the kid has progressed to the next perplexing stage.

Although parents and grandparents can never progress far beyond the novice stage, we may, with faith, effort, and luck, become adequate—but never expert. It is my belief, reinforced by years of "muddling through," that this is all part of a divine plan to teach us to turn always to the Perfect Parent for the needed wisdom and guidance in this, our most important vocation.

> *He will command his angels concerning you to*
> *guard you in all your ways.*

Psalm 91:11

June 18   Parental Pride

It was Eden. In that mythical garden, Adam and Eve enjoyed an adults-only environment: Paradise!

But then the Sly Serpent came on the scene and in the battle that followed, Pride became victor. It should be of note to us parents that it was not until there was a need for humility that, according to the myth, God created human parenthood.

Parental pride is the cause of much sorrow, pain, damage. In its insidious way, it places our own desire to succeed ahead of the welfare of our children and grandchildren. It places undue concern on outward appearances and the opinions of others. It leads to comparisons, competition, and excessive pressure on kids. It often lies at the heart of the rejection of the handicapped and the underachiever and the unattractive.

Parental pride can bring about nervous breakdowns and family breakups and parental burnouts. Its power takes on many disguises, uses imaginative techniques, and causes much family discord. The problems that parental pride can cause know no bounds.

> *Pride goes before destruction,*
> *and a haughty spirit before a fall.*

Proverbs 16:18

June 19   Prerequisite?

I never wanted to be a mother," the woman explained.

"I knew years ago that I did not have a call to motherhood and so decided that I would not have any children. That was the right decision for me.

"But now that my nieces and nephews are having babies, I find myself enjoying a grandmother role with these young ones. It's delightful!

"I've discovered that motherhood is not a prerequisite to a great-and-glorious grandmotherhood!"

> *Then little children were being brought to him*
> *in order that he might lay his hands on them*
> *and pray.*

Matthew 19:13

125

Love is inclusive.
    It is non-sexist,
           non-racist,
                non-biased,
                    non-bigoted.
Exclusion and love are mutually contradictory.
Who of God's children can we possibly exclude?

> *Lead a life worthy of the calling to which you have been called, with all humility and gentleness, with patience, bearing with one another in love, making every effort to maintain the unity of the Spirit in the bond of peace.*

Ephesians 4:1-3

Knit one, purl two, yarn over...."

    The baby's birth or the gift's completion—which will occur first?

"Appliqué blue piece first, then the yellow before embroidering...."

All that has gone before has lead to this place, this time, this wait.

We grandmas work to finish the gift, the be-graced effort of our hands: the baby afghan, the painting, the crocheted baptismal outfit, the poem presented in calligraphy, the crib quilt, the latch hook rug, the panel of weaving, the counted cross-stitch picture, the crewel sampler.

The gift will be love-wrapped and ribboned in prayer. Meanwhile, enveloped in a patchwork quilt of memories, we await the ringing of the phone.

> *When a woman is in labor, she has pain, because her hour has come. But when her child is born, she no longer remembers the anguish because of the joy of having brought a human being into the world.*

John 16:21

June 22   Weeping at Weddings

Why do you always cry at weddings, Nana?"

"I guess because I'm sentimental," I answered glibly. But later, recalling that question, I realized that I cry because a wedding is such a faith-filled and courageous event.

Marriages almost always have sad endings. There is, of course, the sadness of divorce, when the promises of the wedding day are put aside and love-visions are declared null and void.

But even when such trauma is avoided, many marriages lack the happiness envisaged on the wedding day.

And for the truly fulfilled marriages that do last "until death do you part," the inheritance of the survivors is a fierce loneliness.

Yet no matter what the odds, love necessitates this act of courage and faith called marriage. And in the presence of such courage and love and faith—I weep.

> *Let us therefore approach the throne of grace with boldness, so that we may receive mercy and find grace to help in time of need.*

Hebrews 4:16

How fortunate that in our daily lives we are not bound by some bureaucratic definition of family.

Yes, family can be defined by bloodlines and marriage relationships. But people in the neighborhood can be adopted into our family; coworkers can become honorary members; and those people with whom we have a common interest or hobby or concern can become included in family relationships.

Family may include people with whom we have a common life-shaping experience, such as college, the armed services, immigration, pilgrimage. Family can be formed by being confronted with similar challenges, such as joining a 12-step program or living with a person suffering from Alzheimer's or having a child in prison.

Family may also include the faith community with whom we worship or the community in which we live. There are those with whom we have a spiritual relationship who are very much "family" to us.

And since we are all children of God, we are truly *all* members of the one family.

> *This is my commandment, that you love one another as I have loved you.*
>
> **John 15:12**

Barb, parent of four and grandmother to a still-growing number, is a self-admitted, publicly-proclaimed worrier. She explains her anxiousness thus: "I've found, through my years of worrying, that the difficulties and disasters I worry about almost never occur. So I've reasoned that if I worry about all the problems I can think of or imagine, then our family will be safe from those occurrences. I consider worry a form of insurance."

Then again, some people consider worry to be the price we pay for our lack of faith.

Are these our choices: To worry about everything or to worry about nothing?

> *The LORD is your keeper;*
> *the LORD is your shade at your right hand.*
> *The sun shall not strike you by day,*
> *nor the moon by night.*
> *The LORD will keep you from all evil;*
> *he will keep your life.*

Psalm 121:5-7

June 25 — Resolutions

I resolve:
    To be pleasant to those who come to see me—and not berate them for when they do not come;

To be appreciative to those who send letters and cards—and not remind them when they forget;

To be gracious to those who present gifts—and not criticize the gifts.

I resolve to be pleasant, appreciative, gracious, good company, so that both young and old will enjoy being with me!

> *A word fitly spoken is like apples of gold in a setting of silver.*

Proverbs 25:11

June 26   Searching

The giving of answers to the child
is no more important
than our own searching
for those answers!

For thus says the LORD to the house of Israel:
Seek me and live.

Amos 5:4

June 27   Single Parents

There are many more single parents in the world than the statistics indicate.

Some people, because of non-marriage, divorce, separation, or death, wear the obvious label of "single parent."

But others struggle without that handy "single parent" label. For, though there is another partner, he or she has abandoned parenthood in favor of alcohol or work or some other distraction.

All parents deserve the support and affirmation of the entire community, for the entire community suffers when a child grows up deprived. And *single* parents are especially deserving of recognition for the tremendous responsibilities which they carry alone.

The world overflows with opportunities for us to practice our grandparenting.

As God's chosen ones, holy and beloved, clothe
yourselves with compassion, kindness, humility,
meekness, and patience....Above all, clothe your-
selves with love, which binds everything together
in perfect harmony.

Colossians 3:12,14

We should take time to smell the roses, or so we are advised. There certainly have been times when I did not stop to smell flowers...or anything else in the vicinity! However, looking back at those times, I realize that had I stopped to evaluate the situation, I would soon have resumed my activities. What I missed by not pausing in my busyness was recognizing that I was doing what I really wanted to do!

Sometimes we need to take time to realize that, underneath the distractions and frustrations of daily life, we really are happy. We need to take time to realize that, in spite of all the hassles—we are doing exactly what we want to do.

It takes conscious effort to be aware of our contentment, happiness, satisfaction. We humans have the ability to be in the midst of a rose garden and not realize where we are!

> *You show me the path of life.*
> *In your presence there is fullness of joy;*
> *in your right hand are pleasures forevermore.*
> **Psalm 16:11**

June 29   "There Was an Old Woman..."

Sometimes I feel like that shoe-residing old woman in the nursery rhyme. Except with me it's having so many grandkids I don't know what to do.

I try to remember their birthdays...but the dates get scrambled.

I try to remember which kids are in which sports and activities...but the seasons change so rapidly.

I try to remember their interests and hobbies and friends...but they keep developing new ones.

I try to remember what grades they are in and which schools they attend...but the years go by so rapidly.

I certainly try to keep track of First Communions and Confirmations and graduations and weddings and divorces and spouses...but it's so confusing.

Sometimes, when I pray for them, I can't even remember all their names....

> *Even though I walk through the darkest valley,*
> *I fear no evil;*
> *for you are with me;*
> *your rod and your staff—*
> *they comfort me.*

Psalm 23:4

June 30   Recuperation

Children go directly from sick to well without ever touching the "recuperation" space on the playing board of family life. Therefore they do not understand recuperation, which is an adults-only state.

Anyone not convinced of this should try recuperating in a house full of youngsters.

> *The glory of youths is their strength,*
> *but the beauty of the aged is their gray hair.*

Proverbs 20:29

An airport is a delightful place for people-watching:
Business people, presenting opportunities for occupation-guessing;

Vacationers, leaving with high expectations or returning frustrated or fulfilled;

People of all ages, traveling home for holidays or other family times—both happy and sad;

Divorced parents, awaiting the visitation of their children;

Students, anxiously leaving for school, wearily returning or excitedly going on break;

Waiting families, welcoming adopted children from other cities, other countries;

Grandparents, going to or coming from weddings or graduations, First Communions or Confirmations, the introduction to new grandchildren.

At the airport, the exuberant welcomes and the tearful, extended good-byes all express love. Maybe we should all attend "airport" every week.

> ***The LORD will keep your going out and your coming in
> from this time on and forevermore.***
>
> **Psalm 121:8**

Beauty surrounds us with a universal language and reminders of God, who *is* Beauty. Nature reflects the Creator's splendor: the daily hello/good-bye of the sun; wooded solitudes; star-filled skies; flowers worth hallowing. Imagination and engineering create beauty of mathematical conciseness, according to the Creator's physical laws. Beauty is in the predictable forms of a Bach fugue or a Shakespeare sonnet; the simplicity of a Picasso sketch or the radiant color of an O'Keeffe painting or the detailing of a Michelangelo sculpture; the loveliness of a Graham ballet or the emotional impact of Beethoven's Ninth.

There is the beauty of home, of furnishings that bid us welcome and meals that communicate love. There is the beauty of faith, of being one with others in the praise of God, partaking in rituals old and new. There is the beauty of humanity's diversity: the new-to-life; the old on heaven's threshold; the different, awakening us to new insights; the poor, sharing their need with us; the mentally disabled, teaching us; the physically disabled, alerting us to our own limitations; the totality of God's children.

What a privilege to help introduce the young to beauty.

> *Out of Zion, the perfection of beauty,*
> *God shines forth.*

Psalm 50:2

July 3   Comfort Zones

What a variety of *comfort zones* we enjoy!

Some of us are comfortable in a school environment with books and chalk-dust; some prefer the environment of merchandise-for-sale or the office with its information exchange.

Others define a comfort zone by the unique smells and sounds of a hospital or the legalese of a court room or the chaos of the stock exchange. Some prefer the familiarity of a home or the openness of the outdoors, the activity of kids-in-abundance or the presence of food-to-be-cooked and served.

Each of us has a surroundings preference: things-to-be-cleaned or fixed or driven; computers, music, art, animals, books, plants; babies or kids or adults or the elderly or the disadvantaged.

Each of us has a preference for our larger environment: metropolitan area, city, suburb, small town, rural; mountains, valleys, seashore, lakeside, forest, desert; rainy or arid or temperate climate.

How exciting to see the many varied opportunities that our grandchildren—and especially our granddaughters—now have to search out their own comfort zones!

Do everything for the glory of God.

1 Corinthians 10:31

July 4   Freeing Love

Today our country celebrates our many glorious freedoms! Today is therefore an opportune time to consider the freeing aspects of love:

Love, being of God, is always life-giving.

Love never smothers or binds but is always nurturing and empowering.

Love frees the one loved to be fully and gloriously the person God created.

> *If you continue in my word, you are truly my disciples; and you will know the truth, and the truth will make you free.*

John 8:31-32

July 5   Dependents

The awkward, noisy, juvenile birds, ineffective at foraging for food, pecked unsuccessfully at the ground. They copied the motions of their parents, but either scratched too shallow or dug too deep or simply didn't recognize the eatables. Their loud squawking and wildly flapping wings indicated their frustration and hunger.

Their overworked parents, driven by instinct, knew that their young, though able to fly and already larger in size than mom and dad, were not yet independent. And so these smaller, weary birds continued feeding their clamoring offspring.

Do parent birds feel harried as they reach up, again and again, to place the food into the gaping beaks of their already adult-size young?

"Aren't these kids ever going to leave the nest and give us some peace?"

> *Love is patient; love is kind....It bears all things, believes all things, hopes all things, endures all things.*
>
> **1 Corinthians 13:4,7**

July 6   Dieting

At this time in our lives we grandmas have finally freed ourselves from the arbitrary standards of female beauty imposed upon us by society. We ignore the skinny models placed before us; we reject the dieting made necessary by the latest styles and fads. Surely God intended us to broaden physically as well as mentally and spiritually as we age.

But our freedom is fleeting. Now we are victims of dieting dictated by health concerns. Our reluctant vigilance, meager discipline, and ever-present guilt continue.

Perhaps our consolation is to be found in the realization that we have the luxury to be selective in our eating—whatever the reason—while much of the world struggles against starvation and malnutrition.

As we purchase more special-diet cookbooks, clip healthy lifestyle recipes, watch calories and cholesterol and whatever, let us remember, in prayer and action and almsgiving, those who have no food.

Dieting is a luxury!

> *I was hungry and you gave me food,*
> *I was thirsty and you gave me something to*
> *drink.*

Matthew 25:35

July 7   Errant Flakes

Some mornings it just happens. As I pour milk on my cereal, the stream of liquid hits a flake that is positioned wrong and there goes milk all over the tablecloth!

One errant flake makes a mess of the table, puts me in a bad mood, causes me to be late for work, and just possibly disrupts the course of my entire day.

Have I really yielded all that power to one cornflake?

> *God is a God not of disorder but of peace.*

1 Corinthians 14:33

July 8   Family Traits

Heredity is so unpredictable.

Sometimes traits are obviously passed on from parent to child: "Like father, like son"; "She's just like her mother." But sometimes those traits leapfrog a generation; they pass from grandparent to grandchild, leaving a bewildered middle generation bracketed by a matching pair.

> *Every creature loves its like, and every person*
> *the neighbor. All living beings associate with*
> *their own kind, and people stick close to those*
> *like themselves.*

Sirach 13:15-16

July 9   A Cup of Tea, a Bath, a Prayer

My respite, my source of energy and tranquility: a cup of tea, a bath, a prayer.

Life's difficult decisions seem less intimidating when faced with a cup of tea, a bath, a prayer.

My mistakes diminish in gravity when examined with a cup of tea, a bath, a prayer.

My failures lose their sense of finality when contemplated with a cup of tea, a bath, a prayer.

My needs become simpler when considered with a cup of tea, a bath, a prayer.

The future becomes less threatening when braved with a cup of tea, a bath, a prayer.

God's loving and merciful presence is encountered, acknowledged, celebrated with a cup of tea, a bath, a prayer.

> *Those of steadfast mind you keep in peace—*
> *in peace because they trust in you.*

Isaiah 26:3

July 10   Girl Scout Handbook

Nana, your old Girl Scout handbook is soooo funny!

"Look! Here it talks about manners and it says you shouldn't monopolize the *radio* at home. It doesn't even mention TV.

"And the U.S. flag—it only has forty-eight stars!

"And Nana, what is a *runabout child*?

"And dues of three cents a week.

"And the pictures!
"And Nana...."

> *See, the former things have come to pass, and
> new things I now declare.*

Isaiah 42:9

July 11   Graciousness

Love is giving generously—coupled with the often more demanding task of receiving graciously.

Love never denies another the opportunity to give.

> *Show by your good life that your works are
> done with gentleness born of wisdom.*

James 3:13

July 12   Handwriting

Prized possessions come in many forms: I treasure my grandmother's recipes.

Of course, the whole family values those recipes for the delectable bread, salsa, rice and beans that they make possible.

But these recipes are not magazine or newspaper cutouts; nor were they copied or typed on a machine. Abuela copied these recipes in her own handwriting.

Those cards are holy relics, for when I place my fingers on them I am touching my own grandmother, and through her, all people of the past.

The righteous walk in integrity—
happy are the children who follow them!

Proverbs 20:7

July 13   Holy Moments

Mr. Wren anxiously assessed the neighborhood as a location for a family residence; finally the wooden birdhouse hanging from our backyard clothesline pole was chosen. Then followed long days during which the love-sick Mr. Wren sang his heart out—proclaiming his territory and his longing for Mrs. Wren. Eventually a suitable pairing occurred and the nest building began. The eggs were laid. There was relative quiet. One day the parents' frantic activity began. We watched out the windows as Mr. and Mrs. Wren carried food to the hungry little ones; we watched while seated in the backyard lawn chairs or around the picnic table; sometimes we watched through binoculars at all the parental exertion. Soon the hungry baby wrens were eagerly poking their heads out the entrance hole.

All this I and my grandkids had observed.

Finally the time arrived, and we were there! Over several hours, the five fledgling wrens took their maiden flights. One, to our utter amazement, landed on the picnic table in our midst. The bird looked around with curiosity at where his uncontrolled first flight had brought him. The grandchildren sat quietly as, with youthful courage, the fledgling took off again.

Holy moments don't always happen in church.

Make a joyful noise to God, all the earth;
sing the glory of his name;
give to him glorious praise.

Psalm 66:1-2

July 14   "How Are You?"

I t is so easy to slip into the habit of always talking about my health...or lack of it. Sometimes conversations with others my age turn into exchanges of symptoms, medications, surgeries and hospital stays, doctors, physical therapy routines, types of wheelchairs, nursing techniques, and life-limiting experiences.

Although I may find it difficult to believe, not everyone regards my state of health as fascinating a topic of conversation as I do.

And I must remember that not everyone who asks "How are you?" really wants an honest, graphic, complete answer to that question.

> *My flesh and my heart may fail,*
> *but God is the strength of my heart and my*
> *portion forever.*

Psalm 73:26

July 15   Immediately—If Not Sooner

T he winner of an election is announced before all the balloting has taken place; a phone call puts us in instantaneous communication with people anywhere on earth— and even beyond; a click of a camera—and there's the picture. As we become accustomed to split-second results, however, we may lose appreciation for the joys and the rewards that can come only from patient attention to time-consuming and discipline-demanding tasks. In our search for instant gratification we deny ourselves opportunities for the practice of virtues like patience and faith, and especially the patience and faith that are integral parts of love.

All this immediacy intensifies the difficulties of parenting today, for if anything requires patience and faith it is that. Not simply the patience of the now—wiping up the spilled milk of the toddler or waiting out the late hour of the teenager with the car—but the patience that sustains a parent's dedication to this difficult vocation when gratifying results are long absent.

Fortunately this kind of sustained patience and faith can be abundantly fostered by the faithful support of a parent's mom.

> *Those who wait for the LORD shall renew their strength, they shall mount up with wings like eagles, they shall run and not be weary, they shall walk and not faint.*

Isaiah 40:31

July 16   In-and-Out

Young children very often *go* in-and-out.
Older children very often *move* in-and-out.
But no matter where they are, our offspring have a way of trespassing on our lives, our time, our hearts.

> *For you shall go out in joy, and be led back in peace; the mountains and the hills before you shall burst into song, and all the trees of the field shall clap their hands.*

Isaiah 55:12

July 17   Kitchens

My living room is nicely furnished and well coordinated.
My family room is comfortable and homey.
My porch is sunny and cheery.

Yet we always congregate in the kitchen, for it is in the kitchen that we are *eucharist* for one another.

It is in the kitchen where we get nourishment for our bodies and for our souls.

It is in the kitchen where we feed one another with our words and hugs and stories and food.

It is in the kitchen where we, as members of the Body of Christ, are one. We are eucharist for one another!

> *Then he took a loaf of bread, and when he had given thanks, he broke it and gave it to them, saying, "This is my body, which is given for you. Do this in remembrance of me." And he did the same with the cup after supper, saying, "This cup that is poured out for you is the new covenant in my blood."*

Luke 22:19-20

July 18   Prayer for My Family

O God, Source of All Good,
in wisdom you created families
to be expressions of your love.

Bless us with your abundant grace
that we may accept one another
as you accept us.
Bless us with your never-failing mercy
that we may forgive one another
as you forgive us.
Bless us with your empowering spirit
that we may love one another
as you love us.

And when all has been done
bring us to our eternal home,
that we may be united with you

in the onc family of everlasting love.
> *May mercy, peace, and love be yours in abun-*
> *dance.*

Jude 2

July 19   Love's Heart

Love directs,
    guides,
    assists
us parents and grandparents.
And love gives
the child
a heart
forgiving of our mistakes.
> *A new heart I will give you, and a new spirit I*
> *will put within you; and I will remove from*
> *your body the heart of stone and give you a*
> *heart of flesh.*

Ezekiel 36:26

July 20   Not Quite Rihgt

Some days, nothing is quite rihgt.
    Dishes braek;
    Clothess get stained;
  Peoble are late;
  Hose nur;
  Tasks are forgetten;
  Files are mistfiled;

Messages get gabbled;
Everyting is out-of-ordre.
HWY?

> *Why are you cast down, O my soul,*
> *and why are you disquieted within me?*
> *Hope in God; for I shall again praise him,*
> *my help and my God.*

Psalm 43:5

July 21   Prophets

Parents are called to be prophets to their children, but we grandparents are called to be prophets to two generations. A prophet is one chosen to proclaim God's word; surely we are to proclaim God's word to those entrusted to us. A prophet is an example of response and faithfulness to a divine call; surely we are to be virtuous examples to our young.

Contrary to popular belief, however, a prophet does not necessarily have visions of the future; rather a prophet is one who sees the reality of the now. We need to be in touch with reality so that we can speak of the present, for we know from experience that—except for those rare times when God directly intervenes in time—the future proceeds quite naturally from the present.

And so we may, like the biblical prophets, be called to confront those around us. But we do so cautiously, recalling the usual grim response of the people to those prophets of old. We do our confrontations with a gentle touch, with a bit of humor, with loving kindness, lest we find ourselves suffering the harsh fate common to so many prophets.

> *Then Jesus said to them, "Prophets are not with-*
> *out honor, except in their hometown, and*
> *among their own kin, and in their own house."*

Mark 6:4

July 22   Presents

A *present* is a gift anyone can give.

The present is the gift of potential miracles given to us by God.

But the unique present only we can give our young is *our presence.*

> **My presence will go with you.**
> **Exodus 33:14**

July 23   They

W henever we think that what we do is not important, we need to recall that we are the *they* to everyone else.

> *But a Samaritan...was moved with pity. He went to him and bandaged his wounds, having poured oil and wine on them. Then he put him on his own animal, brought him to an inn, and took care of him.*
>
> **Luke 10:33-34**

July 24   Waiting for the Future

W aiting for the future is one of the world's most effective enticements to the insidious and regrettable habit of ignoring the wonder of this moment, this day, this child.

We parents wait for birth, ignoring the miracle of conception and pregnancy. We wait for the child to be toilet trained, to reach school age, to be of driving age, so we will have the perfect opportunities to do, say, go, see, visit. We wait to be independent of parenting. Then we await grandparenting.

Just as there are no perfect times to have a child, so too there are no perfect opportunities during either parenthood or grandparenthood. There are only gilt-edged moments, masquerading as inconveniences, interruptions, frustrations.

Viewing such occasions through loving eyes of faith helps in the recognition of priceless opportunities.

> *All the works of the LORD are very good, and whatever he commands will be done at the appointed time....From the beginning to the end of time he can see everything, and nothing is too marvelous for him.*

Sirach 39:16, 20

July 25   Zoo

There are two common definitions of "zoo":

    (1)   A place where wild and dangerous animals reside;

    (2)   A home with several children.

The facility named second lacks both the safeguards and the organization of the facility referred to in definition one.

> *In you, O LORD, I take refuge.*

Psalm 71:1

Of course I miss the people! I miss seeing them, exchanging the pleasantries that are common among coworkers, trading news of families and hobbies and all the various facets of our lives. I miss our bus rides and coffee breaks, our lunches and celebrations. I miss that "at home" feeling I had at work.

On the other hand, I've discovered new kinds of freedom: I no longer have to plan my household tasks and errands for after work or days off; my outdoor activities, while still dependent upon the fickleness of the weather, can be easily rescheduled; family visits and travel can be planned for any time of the year; I have energy for creative projects and ventures; I have ample opportunities for all that volunteer work that I previously had to avoid. I even have the freedom to be busier than when I worked!

I have retired *from* my job and retired *to* the next phase of my life.

> *I am about to do a new thing; now it springs forth, do you not perceive it?*
>
> **Isaiah 43:19**

It is cuteness that stops just this side of embarrassment: John and Elizabeth are in love. It is "Johnny Dear" and "My Precious Lizzie"; "Honey" and "Sweetheart" and "Darling." Each seems incomplete when the other is not present.

But John and Elizabeth are not adolescents—unless there is a post-menopausal version. They are both widowed, survivors from first marriages that, to most of us observers, seemed much different from the present one.

John and Elizabeth are not the first couple to find an entirely new kind of closeness following termination of their first marriages. And, I wonder, is this new relationship due in part to the differences in their paired personalities? Or does their mutual appreciation exist because they individually have survived death—either of a spouse or of a marriage? Is it because they have suffered the loneliness and solitude which follow such loss that they willingly risk this new vulnerability?

> *Happy are those who find wisdom,*
> *and those who get understanding.*
>
> **Proverbs 3:13**

July 28   The Sisterhood

The *Brotherhood's* long domination of the world is at last being challenged by the *Sisterhood*. Our aim is not to replace one controlling group with another, but to change the whole world.

We seek mutuality, not control; we demand equality of all; we call for compassionate justice. We explore new images of family and government and church and society; we strive for new models for businesses and institutions; we search for different heroes; we offer new paradigms for relationships and nonviolent solutions to problems. We promote long-ignored images of the Divine; we celebrate the sacramentality of everyday life; we recognize the sacredness of the earth and our bodies and all living things.

We value the experience of all—including women and children; we treasure intuition and imagination along with rationality; we assert that each of us is an integrated person composed of body and soul that cannot be divided. We search for an end to poverty and ignorance and every lack; we seek the means for all to live safely; we celebrate both our worldwide diversity and our membership in the universal family of God.

We sisters have begun a tremendous task. But look how much we've already accomplished!

> *Your light shall break forth like the dawn.*

Isaiah 58:8

July 29   Cheated

I t used to be the parents who disciplined the kids. The grandparents were expected to spoil them.

But somewhere along the way, the rules changed.

Today many parents are doing the spoiling and we grandparents, who learned by the old rules, are left once again with the disciplining.

We feel cheated.

> *Hear, my child, your father's instruction,*
> * and do not reject your mother's teaching;*
> *for they are a fair garland for your head,*
> * and pendants for your neck.*

Proverbs 1:8-9

July 30   Television: Nay!

T V is a noisome wasteland!

The news programs focus on the sensational and spectacular, not the truly newsworthy. The media is obsessed with whatever is graphic, startling, colorful, or controversial—not on what needs to be communicated.

TV is filled with violence, with sex that is removed from morality or responsibility, with humor that is demeaning.

TV makes heroes of sports personalities, talk show hosts, actors—with no concern for what kind of examples they offer to the young.

And those annoying ads! While insulting our intelligence, they advocate a lifestyle absorbed with materialism.

TV portrays such a distorted view of life that if all my experience of the world were dependent upon it, I'd never leave my apartment or unlock my doors.

I hate TV!

> *In those days there was no king in Israel; all the*
> *people did what was right in their own eyes.*
>
> **Judges 21:25**

July 31   Television: Yea!

TV is wonderful!

It is a treasure trove of information. The educational channels present in-depth news programs and analyses and documentaries so that I am in touch with significant happenings everywhere.

The nature programs present me with such unbelievable images of animals and wildlife and scenery. And the travelogs enable me to visit incredible places in the world—and even some out of this world.

I have at my fingertips exciting, restful and uplifting music and plays, ballet, opera and comedy. They are such welcome visitors to my home.

And all those marvelous movies! One day I watch a golden oldie, the next day a recent release.

TV distracts me from loneliness and provides entertainment, education, inspiration.

I love TV!

> *We know that all things work together for good*
> *for those who love God.*

Romans 8:28

August 1   Aliens

Sometimes, when I look at the young, I see them as aliens living in a foreign land.

We have produced a culture that is often hostile to our children. We surround them with a violent society; we rob them of their childhood innocence; we transgress the boundaries of youth by imposing harsh life experiences; we kill their faith in adults and in the future.

We lure them unsuspectingly with a sophistication far beyond their comprehension; we reserve nothing of adulthood from them, even though they have not the tools to deal with such experiences. Surely they are aliens in our land.

Scripture tells us to be especially compassionate to aliens.

> **You shall not oppress the alien. The alien who
> resides with you shall be to you as the citizen
> among you; you shall love the alien as yourself.**
> **Leviticus 19:33-34**

August 2   Prayer of the Busy Life

God of Time and Energy,
You who can do all things—
I have too much to do.

You know my complaints about all this activity:
At times I resent the demands others make of me;
How I long for more quiet, more stillness, more peace.

But you and I both know
that much of my busyness is of my own making.
My busyness assures me I'm still needed;

My busyness convinces me I'm not through living life.

Thank you, God, for my busyness!
> *She looks well to the ways of her household,*
> *and does not eat the bread of idleness.*

Proverbs 31:27

August 3   Back to School

The "Back to School" sales are in full hype; the store displays are packed with school supplies, uniforms, clothes.

No matter how old our kids—or our grandkids—we never outgrow our need to be interested in our schools and teachers and youth ministers and the world of the young.

From the beginning of human existence, no society or culture has been, or ever will be, more than one generation removed from being savages.

> *The good leave an inheritance to their children's*
> *children.*

Proverbs 13:22

August 4   Being a Woman

The woman physician said to her audience of both men and women, "It is my wish that every man could experience one menstrual period, one labor pain, and one hot flash." The women in the audience cheered.

I cheered loudest. All three experiences are history for me!

> *There was a woman who had been suffering*
> *from hemorrhages for twelve years; and though*
> *she had spent all she had on physicians, no one*

could cure her. She came up behind (Jesus) and touched the fringe of his clothes, and immediately her hemorrhage stopped....He said to her, "Daughter, your faith has made you well; go in peace."

Luke 8:43-44,48

August 5   Coming...and Going

I love my grandchildren—I really do.

I look forward to seeing them, visiting with them, finding out what's new in their lives—I really do.

And I'm glad to see them leave—I really am.

> *Rejoice always, pray without ceasing, give thanks in all circumstances.*

1 Thessalonians 5:16-18

August 6   Discouragement

There are times in the course of family relationships and work and community involvement when happiness and fulfillment and contentment are non-existent; there are times in the course of life when it seems that its purpose is to drive us to despair.

And that may be right! Sometimes we need to be driven off the brink of despair and plunged into the reality of God; sometimes we need to be stripped of everything, except faith.

And only then, when nearly all else is gone, can faith fill the vacuum within us. Then we discover ourselves a little closer to the Creator of Life—the Creator of our lives and of all those around us.

> *The steadfast love of the LORD never ceases,*
> *his mercies never come to an end;*
> *they are new every morning;*
> *great is your faithfulness.*

Lamentations 3:22-23

August 7   Daughters and Sons

I have daughters and sons who are family because of the love that their father and I have for each other. We call each a daughter or a son.

I have daughters and sons who are family because of the love our daughters and sons have for them. We call each a daughter-by-love or a son-by-love.

Love has ways of bringing new life into a family.

> *So (Naomi) said, "See, your sister-in-law has*
> *gone back to her people and to her gods; return*
> *after your sister-in-law." But Ruth said, "Do not*
> *press me to leave you or to turn back from fol-*
> *lowing you! Where you go, I will go; Where you*
> *lodge, I will lodge; your people shall be my peo-*
> *ple, and your God my God."*

Ruth 1:15-16

August 8   The Sunflower

The sight before us as we looked over the bridge rail was at once incongruous and inspiring. In the median strip be-tween the lanes of highway was a tall, perhaps six-foot-high, sunflower, defiantly in full bloom.

The traffic zoomed past, at fifty-five miles per hour or more, with each vehicle creating such air turbulence that the yellow head shook violently in its own private tornado.

Yet there it stood in that most barren of concrete environments. Somehow its seed had found soil in a small crack, taken root in the unseen ground, and grown. It had weathered the twenty-four-hours-a-day, seven-days-a-week traffic.

Not only had it survived—it flourished magnificently!

> *The earth is full of the steadfast love of the*
> LORD.

Psalm 33:5

August 9   Babies

What is it about babies?
    Is it their size, their cuddliness, their cuteness?
    Is it their dependence and vulnerability?
Is it their potential? The vast future that awaits them?
Is it the mystery of life which they embody?
Is it that they remind us of God's presence and love?
Is it that they are visible signs of faith?
Is it that they reflect God's faith in humanity and
    humanity's faith in God?
What is it about babies?

> *God said to Abraham, "As for (Sarah) your wife*
> *....I will bless her and she shall give rise to na-*
> *tions; kings of peoples shall come from her."*

Genesis 17:15,16

August 10   Family Trees

There are sections of Scripture that are almost universally considered boring: the infamous "begots." Yet what we today deem skippable the Scripture writers considered significant, for they knew that a person's family history often revealed much about that individual.

The modern form of the "begots" is the family tree. But future genealogists will certainly be faced with a formidable task when attempting to construct some present-day family trees.

There is, of course, divorce's tree-splitting lightning stroke; there are the graftings of remarriage with its blending of families; there are the independent sproutings of single parent families; there are modern variations to family trees in same sex parents and test-tube babies and surrogate mothers.

All types of family trees, from the deeply rooted to the most fragile, are important. Each influences a young child and thereby impacts society and the world. Within this diversity of "begots" we still find myriad opportunities to express our love for God and humanity.

> *I am the vine, you are the branches. Those who*
> *abide in me and I in them bear much fruit.*
>
> **John 15:5**

August 11   Life With Teenagers

I still recall a conversation I had years ago with our pediatrician. We were discussing teenagers. The doctor, a very warm, sympathetic woman, shook her head in utter frustration. "Nothing in all my education and training prepared me for the experience of being the mother of four teenagers!"

But let all who take refuge in you rejoice;
let them ever sing for joy.
Spread your protection over them,
so that those who love your name may exult
in you.
For you bless the righteous, O LORD;
you cover them with favor as with a shield.
Psalm 5:11-12

August 12   Giving

We give our kids so much! Sometimes, however, forget to point out to the young that *giving* is also one of the keys to happiness. We must not forget to give them opportunities to give.

And he said to them, "Pay attention to what you
hear; the measure you give will be the measure
you get, and still more will be given you."
Mark 4:24

August 13   How Must I Love?

Love is not
If not from my heart.
Yet that does not suffice.

Love must be
My soul's entity.
Yet more is still required.

Strong is love!
Empow'red is this love
That's being sought from me.

Love from mind's
Most treasuring finds
Is part of this command.

Love must I
My neighbor as I?
This love must know no bounds!

> *You shall love the LORD your God with all your
> heart, and with all your soul, and with all your
> strength, and with all your mind; and your
> neighbor as yourself.*

Luke 10:27

August 14   Heart Blessing

My heart is such a wonderful creation. This powerful and
efficient muscle has been beating since before my birth,
setting the rhythm of each day of my life.

Without conscious effort on my part, it beats; without direction
from me, it beats; whether I am awake or asleep, it beats, nourish-
ing my entire body.

My heart, a symbol of love, is kind to me. In appreciation of my
heart, I think kind thoughts, refusing to add stress to this organ of
mine. In consideration of my heart, I relax, releasing tension and
anxiety, freeing my heart to do its task without restriction or limi-
tation.

Today, and everyday, I gratefully bless my heart.

The LORD is my strength and my shield;
in him my heart trusts;
so I am helped, and my heart exults,
and with my song I give thanks to him.

Psalm 28:7

August 15   Mary

Why was there a Mary? Why didn't an adult Christ just appear on earth and immediately begin his ministry? Would that really have made a difference?

It is the crucifixion scene that answers my questions, for Mary is there. It is as the mother of the crucified one that she was called upon to forgive—not only the crucifiers of her son but also the God who had "tricked" her. Wasn't this man on the cross the one who was to occupy the throne of David and rule over the house of Jacob, Mary must have wondered. How could this happen to the Son of God? Yet even in her agonized questioning she remained faithful.

There was a Mary in salvation history to be a model for us: to those of us who have sat by the bedside of a sick or dying child; to every parent who has lost a child through the brutal or irresponsible actions of another; to all of us who have accepted the challenges of life in good faith and have been "tricked" by God; to all of us called upon to forgive—not just those who scourge or reject or crucify us, but those who torment or reject those whom we love; to all of us, for we are all called to a faith of forgiveness.

Do not judge, and you will not be judged;
do not condemn, and you will not be con-
demned. Forgive, and you will be forgiven;
give, and it will be given to you.

Luke 6:37-38

161

August 16 "Knowing"

While sex is an integral part of Scripture, the ancient writers refrained from indulging in explicit sex scenes. And in place of biological terms or slang, Scripture writers used the term "knowing" to refer to having sex. As Mary said to the Archangel Gabriel when told she was to bear a child, she "did not *know* man."

One of the truly pleasurable aspects of sex between the long-married is that we "know" each other. We know what pleases our partner; we "know" the "right fit"; we "know" each other's body; we "know" the stretch marks and love handles and scars; we "know" the turn-ons and the turn-offs; we "know" each other.

It is a "knowing" accompanied with pleasure and surprise and ecstasy and commitment. And oh, what passion!

> *Arise, my love, my fair one, and come away; for now the winter is past, the rain is over and gone. The flowers appear on the earth; the time of singing has come, and the voice of the turtle-dove is heard in our land.*

Song of Solomon 2:10-12

August 17 "Made by God"

Look, Grandma! See what we made in school today!" On his shirt my grandson wore a colorfully decorated paper shield:

"What's the matter, Grandma? Why are you crying—don't you like it?"

"Oh Anthony! I like it very much. I wish everyone in the whole wide world wore a sign like that. The world would be much different, Anthony, if we recognized that each one of us is made by God."

> *Here I am;*
> *in the scroll of the book it is written of me.*
>
> **Psalm 40:7**

August 18   Impressing Others

I must admit that there have been times when I've sought to impress people. Through pride or self-aggrandizement, I've tried to appear more competent or capable than I really am...and have usually fallen flat on my face.

But there have been other times in my life when, faced with all-consuming challenges or difficulties, I've completely forgotten about what others might think. At such times I had no choice but to stop worrying about impressing others and simply do what I thought was right.

Later—often many years later—I discovered that's when the various people-watchers in my life most closely focused on my actions. And, occasionally, it was at those times, when I could not spare a thought to others' evaluations, that—to my amazement—I did impress people.

> *All who exalt themselves will be humbled,*
> *and all who humble themselves will be exalted.*
>
> **Matthew 23:12**

August 19 — My Kids

My kids, grown adults with children of their own, will always be my *kids*.

No matter how capable or well-educated they become, in my mind, they will always be my *kids*.

No matter how prestigious, how famous or respected they become, they will always be my *kids*.

No matter how significant their achievements, they will always be my *kids*.

And, should my stay here on earth extend until I am one of the "very elderly" and they themselves are old and retired, they will remain my *kids*.

> *I have been young, and now am old.*
>
> **Psalm 37:25**

August 20 — Words of Wisdom

People who have overcome challenges or survived ordeals or attained great success often credit their accomplishments to the wisdom of a parent or grandparent:

"I remember the words of my father..." or

"My mother always said..." or

"My grandparents used to tell me...."

My own curiosity always prompts me to wonder about such a statement. How I'd relish being able to inquire directly of that wisdom's source: "Did you actually say that? More than once?"

I then wonder further: What words of mine do others remember?

> *For as the rain and the snow come down from heaven, and do not return there until they have watered the earth, making it bring forth and*

*sprout, giving seed to the sower and bread to the
eater, so shall my word be that goes out from my
mouth; it shall not return to me empty, but it
shall accomplish that which I purpose, and succeed in the thing for which I sent it.*

Isaiah 55:10-11

August 21   Problems?

It has been said that God never regards us as problems. To
God, we are always possibilities.

Is there a *possibility* that I could take that same attitude toward others?

*Day by day, as they spent much time together in
the temple, they broke bread at home and ate
their food with glad and generous hearts, prais-
ing God and having the goodwill of all the people.*

Acts 2:46-47

August 22   "One Size Fits All"

It used to be so simple. Need diapers? Go buy them.

But that was in the past. Now, of course, it is assumed that
if you are buying diapers you surely want disposables. And is
that a simple task? No!

"Did you want diapers for a baby boy or a baby girl?"

"And how much does the child weigh?"

"Do you want the diapers for daytime or nighttime use?"

"Would you like pull-up style diapers?"
"Regular or ultra-slims?"
"What quantity?"
"Sorry, but they're out of stock."

> *No one can say, "What is this?" or "Why is*
> *that?"—for everything has been created for its*
> *own purpose.*

Sirach 39:21

August 23   "Party, Party!"

Hattie's kids went all out for Hattie's eightieth birthday, putting on a party with decorations and flowers and music and a large cake with exactly eighty candles.

But the party was such a delightful success because of all the people who attended. Hattie's former coworkers were there, and the friends she has made through her kids, and former neighbors and neighbors' children, and out-of-town relatives.

It was a wonderful gathering, celebrating life and friendships and family and community.

A few weeks later Hattie surprised her kids by calling a formal family meeting. The kids assembled in apprehension as she began. "I have a request, and I sincerely hope you will consider it seriously," she said.

They waited nervously. Finally Hattie continued: "I want another party—soon!"

> *Go, eat your bread with enjoyment,*
> *and drink your wine with a merry heart;*
> *for God has long ago approved what you do.*

Ecclesiastes 9:7

August 24   "This Ole Bod!"

This ole bod—she ain't what she used to be!"

Inside I may feel young, but my getting-out-of-bed creaks and moans testify to my eldering. However, some things are still worth doing, even if they do result in groans:

puttering in the garden;
dancing at weddings;
passionate lovemaking;
gatherings of friends;
visiting the grandkids;
helping others;
picnicking;
shopping for gifts;
volunteering;
taking the grandkids on an outing;
traveling;
hobbying;
. . .
. . .

> *A tranquil mind gives life to the flesh.*
> **Proverbs 14:30**

August 25   "Wasting" Time

In this era of efficiency consciousness we wisely strive to make the best use of our time. However, relationships are not always subject to efficiency guidelines.

On occasion, the time we spend with our grandkids seems to be wasted; there is no tangible reward. Yet our willingness just to "be there" conveys irrefutably to the child: "I think you are so important that I am willing to waste time with you." And it is this that they will remember.

We can't always have insightful conversations with children; can't guarantee times filled with warm relations; can't schedule the unfolding of either past hurts or dreams of the future. These require the unique confluence of emotion and environment, readiness and receptivity. They require even more than "quality" time together, for only if we are willing to waste time with the young will we be on hand for those rare "diamond moments" that will live forever in the memories of both adult and child.

> *I will walk among you, and will be your God,*
> *and you shall be my people.*

Leviticus 26:12

August 26   Retreat

No matter how harried my life, I can make a retreat. No matter how burdened by responsibilities, I can make a retreat. No matter how restricted my funds, I can make a retreat.

I can get away any day—for moments at a time—for my mini-retreats consist of immersing myself in God's love.

I leave—mentally and emotionally and spiritually—wherever I am. I am still. I remind myself that I am surrounded by God's love. I am so immersed in that love that I cannot point to it—for it is everywhere. Luxuriating in that love, I find refreshment, relaxation, acceptance, inspiration, peace.

In the Divine Silence I am renewed.

> *He said to them, "Come away to a deserted*
> *place all by yourselves and rest a while."*

Mark 6:31

August 27   Self-Esteem

Self-esteem has little to do with accomplishments, talent, intelligence, education, or recognition. I know people who have achieved much, yet their drive is but a frantic search for self-esteem. I know others who, despite limited abilities or opportunities, possess a beautifully developed self-esteem.

Because of our responsibilities to our Creator, to ourselves, and to the entire human race, we are expected to develop our gifts and abilities. However, such efforts rarely increase our self-esteem.

God's self-description, proclaimed with almighty power and justifiable pride, is "I AM WHO I AM." God's self-naming is given without numeration of deeds accomplished or power utilized or titles assumed; it is the expression of infinite self-esteem.

And it is here—in our relationship to the Divine—that we find the true and abundant source of our own self-esteem. We are all children of a loving, caring God. Is not that fact enough to establish firmly our self-worth?

> *See, I have inscribed you on the palms of my*
> *hands.*

Isaiah 49:16

August 28   So Little Needed

My husband and I were planning to spend the day together. But then, as so often happens in our complicated and unpredictable world, important duties for both of us suddenly appeared. I left the house first, knowing that it would be empty when I returned.

Disappointed that our original plans had to be changed, I entered the kitchen feeling rather depressed. But there, on the chalkboard message center, in his familiar handwriting: "I LOVE YOU."

So little is needed to change the mood of an entire day!

Kindness is like a garden of blessings.

Sirach 40:17

August 29 — Step-Parents

We need an entire new collection of fairy tales. We need a library filled with stories and songs and rhymes about devoted, nurturing, loving step-parents.

No more stories of devious and unloving step-parents, of wicked step-mothers and cruel step-fathers, of spiteful step-siblings and even malevolent step-grandmothers.

We need new fairy tales and songs and rhymes of the true magic that has occurred through the love and acceptance shown by step-parents and step-grandparents: by people who realize that love and caring can transform step-relationships as well as blood relationships into stories worth relating.

And we need more real-life models to show that such relationships can and do work.

The steadfast love of the LORD is from everlasting to everlasting on those who fear him, and his righteousness to children's children.

Psalm 103:17

August 30 — Sowers

It was summer and my granddaughter was visiting. "Remember, Grandma, that tough time I had at college this year?" I nodded, recalling numerous expensive collect phone calls.

"Do you know what you said that got me through that mess?"

I swallowed my first response, which would have been "How in heaven's name should I know—after all the many things I said?" Instead, I managed a simple "No, Dear. What was it?"

"You said, 'No matter what happens today, the sun will rise tomorrow.'"

"I'm glad I could offer something helpful," I answered, but the truth was I couldn't even remember uttering those words. Like the sower in the parable, we grandmas know that not every word-seed of ours will take root in the consciousness of the young. But like the sower who continues to scatter the seed, and like the prophets who continue to teach the word of God, we keep trying to communicate, searching for the right thought, in our efforts to help our youth become responsible, caring adults. Should it happen that none of our words take root, possibly our perseverance itself may be the seed that eventually finds fertile ground.

The sower sows the word.

Mark 4:14

August 31   Scuba-Diving

Since my grandson was taking scuba diving, I soon became acquainted with the vocabulary and techniques of the sport.

His instructor took the job seriously, for he was teaching his students how to deal with potentially life-threatening situations. From the first classroom session the students were drilled: Don't panic!

In the pool the students worked as partners and learned the importance of cooperation. They practiced "buddy breathing"—taking turns using only one mouthpiece and air tank to breathe under water, for survival could depend upon such techniques in a crisis.

And over and over the instructor reminded them to breathe evenly; no matter what happened—no matter the surprise or fear or anxiety—they were to breathe evenly.

Don't panic—take care of each other—keep breathing evenly. As my grandson said, "Grandma, that's good advice in the water—or anywhere!"

> *Where can I go from your spirit?...If I ascend to heaven, you are there....If I take the wings of the morning and settle at the farthest limits of the sea, even there your hand shall lead me and your right hand shall hold me fast.*
>
> Psalm 139:7,8,9-10

September 1 — All the Love

All the love
which I have known
is here within me still.

All the love
which I have sown
diminished not my store.

> *But now, dear lady, I ask you, not as though I were writing you a new commandment, but one we have had from the beginning, let us love one another.*

2 John 5

September 2 — Button Box

I remember my grandmother's button box. Although called a button "box," it really was a round tin that ages before had come filled with hard candy.

I recall as a young child running my fingers through the buttons, sweeping them up in my hands, enjoying their multi-textured feel before letting them cascade noisily into the tin. I would sort them by color or shape or size. Sometimes I would lay them out in swirling designs or geometric shapes; occasionally I would toss a handful onto the linoleum to admire the spontaneous art.

I often wondered where each button had been before being relegated to the button box. Least interesting were the new buttons still on store cards, for they had no stories. But surely the one-of-a-kind could have told—if able to speak—fascinating histories. And those gold-colored buttons—could they be real gold? How about all the pearl ones—might not they be genuine? And the rhinestone-studded buttons—surely they were jewels.

Now my grandchildren play in my button "box," which is really a round tin that ages ago came filled with hard candy....

There is nothing new under the sun.

Ecclesiastes 1:9

September 3 — Being Alone

Being alone is not the same as being lonely.
Being alone means I can choose where to travel in my thoughts;
Being lonely means I wish I were journeying with others.
Being alone means I can choose the song I wish to sing;
Being lonely means I feel like a voice crying in the wilderness.
Being alone means I can become lost in creativity;
Being lonely means I feel the isolation of the martyr.
Being alone means I can affirm my belonging to the community;
Being lonely means I feel shut out of the community.
Being alone means I can spend time with God;
Being lonely means I feel far from God.
In aloneness is my oneness with all.

For God alone my soul waits in silence,
for my hope is from him.

Psalm 62:5

September 4 — Commitment

Our commitment is not just to one or several or even many grandchildren; our commitment is not just to our family or our community; our commitment is to our society and to our faith and to our world.

We—humanity—are never more than one generation away from the demise of our culture.

We—Christianity—are never more than one generation away from having our faith become a relic of the past, of interest only to historians.

Civilization, our religion, our society, our culture—none of these is guaranteed beyond the present generation.

Our commitment is to our society and to our faith and to our world.

Our commitment is to all youth and young people.

> ***Choose this day whom you will serve...but as for me and my household, we will serve the LORD.***
>
> **Joshua 24:15**

September 5 — Debts

We owe! Each of us has a debt that we can never completely repay. That debt is to the world.

Our debt is to those who have preceded us on this earth: those who gave us life and faith; those who built this country and its highways and churches and institutions; those who fought for freedom and equality.

Our debt is to those who live with us now on this earth: those who suffer lack; those who have not freedom or opportunity; those who live in fear and ignorance; those who are victims of prejudice and injustice; those in pain and loneliness; those who live their lives unloved.

Our debt is to those who will follow us on this earth: those who will inherit the remnants of our follies and errors; those who will inherit the legacy of our wisdom and faith and vision; those who will begin their life journeys in the places which we now inhabit.

Using our talents and abilities, our time and money, we make our debt payments over our lifetime.

> *He asked Jesus, "And who is my neighbor?"*
> *Jesus replied, "A man was going down from*
> *Jerusalem to Jericho, and fell into the hands of*
> *robbers...."*

Luke 10:29-30

September 6 — Grandkids Are Nondivorceable

Although a divorce means the end of the marriage relationship, no such separation automatically occurs between grandparent and grandchild.

The ties binding me to my grandchild are not severed by a legal procedure; my love for my grandchild is not dissolved with signatures on a paper.

The heritage of the past combined with visions of the future still remain centered in this child of my child.

> *How often have I desired to gather your children*
> *together as a hen gathers her brood under her*
> *wings.*

Luke 13:34

September 7 — Everyone's a Theologian

We are all theologians.

As much as we might attempt to deny it, there is no way we can escape that designation. No matter what our occupation or profession, no matter how we spend our days, no matter our level of education or knowledge of theology, we are theologians.

With our lives, with our words and actions and thoughts, each of us deals with the basic theological questions that humanity has always asked:

Why am I here?

What is the purpose of life?

Who—or what—is my god?

Why is there evil in the world?

Why is there suffering?

What happens after death?

We are all theologians, demonstrating our theology in the most effective way. It is theology—not written or read or discussed—but theology lived.

In him we live and move and have our being.

Acts 17:28

September 8 — Morning Prayer

Thank you, God, for this gloriously unique day— this day that shall be but once in all of time.

I rejoice in your gift of this day—
eagerly accepting it from your hands.
I receive it with the wonderment of a child;
I receive it with the idealism of a young adult;
I receive it with the wisdom of my years;
I receive it with the love in which you give it.

Thank you, God, for this most wondrous day.

O come, let us sing to the LORD;
let us make a joyful noise to the rock of our
salvation!
Let us come into his presence with thanksgiving;
let us make a joyful noise to him with songs of
praise!

Psalm 95:1-2

September 9   Evening Prayer

In the quiet of evening I give you thanks,
ever-renewing God, for this day.

I return to you this day,
to perfect and complete it.

I place in your care all my burdens—
they will await tomorrow.

I place in your care all my loved ones—
keep them in your love.

Thank you, God, for life,
for this day now closing,
for this night.he birds have fledged; the nest is empty.
End of problems?
No!

> *I lie down and sleep; I wake again, for the LORD*
> *sustains me.*

Psalm 3:5

September 10   Free-Flying Birds

The birds have fledged; the nest is empty.
End of problems?
No.

Following years of our encouraging the freedom and independence of our children, we find they now resent *our* freedom and independence.

We are expected to be there for them—as we were when they were young and vulnerable.

We are to maintain them as the center of our lives—as we did when they were nest-dwellers.

We are to be supportive of them—as we were when they were trying out their wings.

They think these things should never change.

> **An educated person knows many things, and
> one with much experience knows what he is
> talking about.**
>
> Sirach 34:9

September 11   9/11

These simple numbers, a nine and an eleven, invoke nightmarish videos continuously replayed; sights and sounds beyond imagining. For some people there are added layers of remembrances: smells, sensations of heat and ash, the presence of terror, searing loss.

9/11 served to unite us, in fear and pain, with much of the world. Many peoples have for decades coexisted with terror, with bombs and landmines, with the reality of family members who "disappeared," with torture and amputation, with the fear of the unwelcome knock that comes late at night. 9/11 was our initiation into that world—a world inhabited by people no less valued than the the 9/11 victims, no less loved by family and friends, no less human.

But "9/11" can also become a signal to work and pray ever harder for universal understanding; it can ignite imaginative solutions to injustice, melt our egotistical righteousness, dispel our casualness toward violence, make us open to the Spirit who can inspire us beyond our limited focus; memories of 9/11 must instill in us visions of world peace. Let us surround not just our friends and our country, but also our enemies and all nations with our vision of love and justice and peace for grandparents, parents and children everywhere.

> *But I say to you that listen, Love your enemies,*
> *do good to those that hate you, bless those who*
> *curse you, pray for those who abuse you.*
>
> Luke 6:27-28

September 12   Heart-Shaped Pillows

Two different funerals.

In each casket someone had placed a heart-shaped pillow covered with rosebuds.

One pillow bore a ribbon marked "Grandma." The flower-covered pillow was placed there by strong, still-growing hands; the weeping of the bereaved spoke of a generously lived, full life, lovingly remembered.

The other pillow bore a ribbon marked "Grandson." The flower-covered pillow was placed there by wrinkled, age-spotted hands; the weeping of the bereaved spoke of a too-brief life, and of the raw, unending pain of the survivors.

Perhaps that second heart-shaped pillow should have been broken in two.

A voice is heard in Ramah, lamentation and bitter weeping. Rachel is weeping for her children; she refuses to be comforted for her children, because they are no more.

Jeremiah 31:15

September 13   "How's Your Head?"

It's not an uncommon question in our family. With an economy of words, "How's your head?" includes all of the following:

How are you—in the ways that matter most?

Are your priorities in order?

What's your mental state?

Are you lonely?

Temporary setbacks aside, are you happy?

If you are "down," do you need help?

Do you realize we love you?

Is God in your life?

Do you believe in God's love for you?

Are you open to God now?

Are you working toward a goal?

Are you learning?

Are you growing?

Are you too busy?

Do you feel too pressured?

How are you relating to other people?

What are you doing for humanity?

Are you helping to make the world a better place?

> *And Jesus increased in wisdom and in years, and in divine and human favor.*

Luke 2:52

September 14   Individually and Personally

Love works individually and personally.
    That's how God loves each of us—
        individually and personally.
That's the only way we can love—
  individually and personally.

> *O LORD, you have searched me and known me.*
> *You know when I sit down and when I rise up;*
>   *you discern my thoughts from far away....*
> *Even before a word is on my tongue,*
>   *O LORD, you know it completely.*
> *You hem me in, behind and before,*
>   *and lay your hand upon me.*

Psalm 139:1-2,4-5

September 15   Mail

Look Mom! Here's mail for ME!"
    All kids love to get mail, so having a "mail-relationship" with grandkids can be an effective way of maintaining contact when grand-relatives are separated by ocean or continent.

To a small child, still in the world-wonder stage, an expensive, satellite-assisted phone call is not the technological marvel that it is to us older folks. But the young do experience the pleasure of having something to hold in their hands.

To an older child, caught up in the business of life, writing a letter takes "too much time." However, receiving a letter is definitely special.

For any grandchild, receiving mail is fun—even if the grandparents are just across town or across the street.

"Look, Dad! It has *my* name on it!"

> *I, Paul, write this greeting with my own hand.*
> *Remember my chains. Grace be with you.*

Colossians 4:18

September 16   My Prayer Book

I have a personal prayer book, a treasured collection of survival aids for good times and bad.

There are prayers I learned as a child and familiar verses from that ancient collection of songs called *The Book of Psalms*. There are other Scripture quotes of faith and consolation and challenge. There are prayers that predate Christianity and connect me with all of humanity. There are new and old prayers that address the feminine attributes of an ever-creating and nurturing God. There are prayers from India that recognize the spark of the Divine that is within us all. There are Native American prayers recognizing God's spirit throughout creation. There are hymn texts from Black spirituals that speak of the intensity of both life and faith. There are Buddhist meditations directing me to the Silence. There are prayers from a multitude of saints, both the canonized saints of ages past and modern saints of today.

All these help me find the thoughts and words of my own prayer, for ultimately it is this heart-prayer that is the union of the human and the Divine.

> *Let the peoples praise you, O God: let all the*
> *peoples praise you.*

Psalm 67:3

September 17 Mom's Last Good Deed

Mom literally died with her boots on," said Alicia. "It had just snowed and she had returned to the house after running errands when she had a fatal stroke. No warning.

"But when I started going through my mother's things, I was amazed. In the packet with her will, her living will, her health care power of attorney form, and her insurance policies was a note: 'Get at least ten copies of my death certificate—you'll need them all.'

"In other drawers and closets were many items neatly boxed and labeled: 'This is for David' or 'I made this for Nancy.'

"Of course, her tending to these details made our tasks much easier. But, more important, she helped us begin to accept her death and to enter into the long process of grieving and readjusting. I think of it as *Mom's Last Good Deed*. With her preparations she testified eloquently that she had come to terms with her own mortality. In facing death head-on, she gave us, her survivors, a tremendous sense of consolation: Mom was ready."

> *Lord, let me know my end,*
> *and what is the measure of my days;*
> *let me know how fleeting my life is.*

> **Psalm 39:4**

September 18 Pets

It's been proven that people with pets live longer than people who do not have pets.

Certainly pets make demands of us with their need for care and feeding and exercising and veterinary visits. And tending to such tasks keeps us busy and distracted from our own problems.

But perhaps the most important aspect of pets is that, in contrast to many of us humans, they let themselves be loved.

> *And God said, "Let the earth bring forth living creatures of every kind: cattle and creeping things and wild animals of the earth of every kind." And it was so. God made the wild animals of the earth of every kind, and the cattle of every kind, and everything that creeps upon the ground of every kind. And God saw that it was good.*

Genesis 1:24-25

September 19   Prodigals

I've heard many priest "fathers" give sermons on the Prodigal Son parable. But how many of us parents could give our own hard-gained insight into that timeless story!

We who have had our own prodigal offspring have lived the long, lonely days of that parable. We know the sorrow and heartache of the waiting times of faith, the perseverance of hope in spite of all outward signs to the contrary.

And because we have endured such times, we know and understand deeply the joy and love that only the prodigal's return can bring.

Because of this, we know, as only such suffering can teach, of God's constant and faithful love for us. If we, mere human parents, can remain faithful in our waiting for our own children, how much more faithful and patient must be God, our Heavenly Parent.

> *But while he was still far off, his father saw him and was filled with compassion; he ran and put his arms around him and kissed him.*

Luke 15:20

September 20   Organized?

As I handed out copies of my report to the committee, some-one remarked, "You are so organized!" I smiled gracious-ly in response, while inwardly thinking, *"Me? Organized?"*
Should I conduct a tour of my chaotic closets and topsy-turvy freezer and jumbled basement shelves and muddled attic? Should I have a home-viewing of my disarrayed drawers and age-yellowed papers and miscellany-filled boxes-under-beds? Should I display the reminders I've received for bills I've forgotten to pay, forms I've neglected to complete, surveys I've lost, and registrations that I overlooked? How about presenting a list of library books lost and meetings forgotten?

All that evidence disproves my organizational ability.

However, there are certain tasks that energize me; there are areas of interest that are important to me; there are goals that give mean-ing and purpose to my life.

When I evaluate my efforts in those categories, I do wonder: Maybe I am organized!

> ***All things should be done decently and in order.***
> **1 Corinthians 14:40**

September 21   We Need Kids!

Kids remind us of the wonders of creation that we otherwise may not notice. As we introduce the young to God's world, we listen to our own words and are reminded of the marvels of that world.

We tell our kids, at the lakeside, that God made the beautiful lake, but it is watching them jump the waves and cavort in the water and pretend to catch that big fish that transforms for us the sterile fact of creation into an emotional response of gratitude for its existence.

We view with kids the evening sky, pointing out constellations and planets and shooting stars—and suddenly we are ourselves overcome with the vastness of the cosmos.

As we watch kids play with a cardboard box or a piece of cloth or empty thread spools or a mound of dirt, we feel our dormant imagination reawakening.

We need children, with their uninhibited love and enthusiasm and creativity and sense of wonder. We need children as much as they need us.

> *Look at the rainbow, and praise him who made it; it is exceedingly beautiful in its brightness. It encircles the sky with its glorious arc; the hands of the Most High have stretched it out.*
>
> Sirach 43:11-12

September 22   Rocking Chair

Where do you feed a baby—if not in a rocking chair? Where do you quiet a rambunctious two-year-old—if not in a rocking chair?

Where do you tell stories—if not in a rocking chair?

Where do you daydream—if not in a rocking chair?

Where do you listen most carefully—if not in a rocking chair?

Where do you wait most patiently—if not in a rocking chair?

Where do you pray most ardently—if not in a rocking chair?

Where do you reminisce—if not in a rocking chair?

Where do you hear the voice of God most clearly—if not in a rocking chair?

> *May God be gracious to us and bless us and make his face to shine upon us.*
>
> Psalm 67:1

To love others,
   to love God,
      both require the recognition of self
as worthy of loving,
as worthy of being loved.

> *I am my beloved's, and his desire is for me.*
> **Song of Solomon 7:10**

September 24   Soap Bubbles

I buy dishwashing detergent in the extra-large, super-economy size container, which I keep in the cupboard. At the sink I have a small, sample-size bottle of the detergent and refill it as needed.

I had come to the realization that when I had a larger bottle at the sink I used the liquid lavishly; but when I dispense from that small container, I use the liquid sparingly. While this is good economy, it is much more important to me than saving a few pennies.

That small bottle is a reminder to me that even those things of the earth which seem to be in abundance are all still finite. Though there may seem to be huge quantities in Mother Nature's giant "cupboard," all are limited and should be used sparingly.

> *I resolved to live according to wisdom, and I*
> *was zealous for the good, and I shall never be*
> *disappointed. My soul grappled with wisdom,*
> *and in my conduct I was strict.*
>
> **Sirach 51:18-19**

September 25   Stones

Stones can be precious without being "precious stones":

There are the skipping stones we pitch onto the water's surface;

There are the multicolored stones we pick up on our country walks;

There are the smooth "fingering" stones that fit so well in our hands;

There are the intriguing stones we want to study;

There are the "lucky stones" that make us feel good;

There are the polished stones we use in crafts.

Many of these stones, when combined with children, become the "building-stones" of childhood and the "corner-stones" of adulthood.

These truly are *precious* stones.

> *(There is) a time to throw away stones, and a time to gather stones together.*
>
> **Ecclesiastes 3:5**

September 26   Gobbled-Up!

There are demands, needs, wants from my parents and in-laws, brothers and sisters and cousins, friends and neighbors; there are demands, needs, wants from my kids; there are demands, needs, wants from my grandkids.

I feel like I'm about to be gobbled-up, about to be devoured by those around me!

I'm searching for a safe, quiet corner in which to find and reclaim *me*.

Be merciful to me, O God, be merciful to me,
for in you my soul takes refuge;
in the shadow of your wings I will take refuge.

Psalm 57:1

September 27   A Grandma Lives Here!

The signs are unmistakable:
    Photos of kids on the refrigerator door;
    A candy dish made of craft sticks;
A drawer filled with hand-lettered greetings;
A hidden store of sweets kept for young visitors;
A handy box of children's books;
Jewelry made of seeds, pine cones, safety pins, or wooden beads;
A scout-made birdfeeder outside the window;
Framed and matted crayon and paint-by-number pictures;
A school workshop-made knick-knack shelf;
A stack of receipts from fund-raising raffles;
A child-made papier-mache bouquet;
A plastic-covered greeting card placemat....
Yep, a busy, loving and loved grandma lives here!
> **Without ceasing, I remember you always in my**
> **prayers.**

Romans 1:9

September 28   This Younger Generation

Grandma, I think it's unfair how so many older people complain about us. I'm tired of hearing bad things about *this younger generation.*"
"Wellll," I stalled.

"Look at it this way. People complain about the music we like and the video games we play and lots of other things we do for entertainment—but those things are available only because older people—who have money and want to make more—produce them.

"And Grandma, the big advertising executives aren't teenagers. But they're the ones who push consumerism.

"And you certainly can't blame us for the condition of the world. Don't forget, you older people have the power. You're the ones in government and the legislatures and big business; you're the ones who have been voting and paying taxes for years.

"So, Grandma, blame us for what we hand on to *our* children and grandchildren, but not for today's world."

> *For they sow the wind, and they shall reap the whirlwind.*

Hosea 8:7

September 29 Towels

Whatever are you doing there, Dear?" I asked my granddaughter, as she held up first one bath towel then another.

"Just running a little test, Grandma," she answered. "I'm holding up each of your towels to the window and, if I can see the apartments across the street through the towel, out it goes."

"Are you telling me my towels are a bit worn?"

"No, Grandma, I'm telling you they're completely worn out."

As the rag pile grew, I had to admit that when change is gradual it's very easy to overlook.

> *For the mountains may depart and the hills be removed, but my steadfast love shall not depart from you, and my covenant of peace shall not be*

removed, says the LORD, who has compassion on you.

Isaiah 54:10

September 30 — The Shower

Welcome, Mother-in-law-to-be!"

This was not a typical pre-wedding shower. Here was a gathering of good friends who had no need of games to pass the time; this group of grandma-age confidants had no need to come together for an ostentatious display of consumerism.

Each woman came bearing gifts: mother-in-law stories of inspiration and humor and insight. The gifts for the guest-of-honor were words-of-wisdom, culled from observation or the experience of pain or joy.

The mother-in-law-to-be was showered—not with material items but with love and good wishes, with blessings, with recipes for successful relationships and hints for happiness. Though the testimonials had varied settings and diverse persona, at the end of all the telling they could be summarized quite easily: Be kind. Love one another.

> *All that you have done for your mother-in-law*
> *since the death of your husband has been fully*
> *told me, and how you left your father and moth-*
> *er and your native land and came to a people*
> *that you did not know before. May the LORD re-*
> *ward you for your deeds, and may you have a*
> *full reward from the LORD, the God of Israel,*
> *under whose wings you have come for refuge!*

Ruth 2:11-12

October 1   Surrounded by Love

In *The Story of a Soul: The Autobiography of Saint Therese of Lisieux,* the saint-in-the-making describes her remarkable childhood.

Therese writes of having been surrounded by love all of her life. Her first memories were of tender caresses and warm smiles. Though her mother died when Therese was only four years old, her four older sisters, led by their father, lovingly provided only good example, to the child. To her father, Therese was "Queen"; and of this extraordinary man Therese writes that all who knew him said he had never been known to speak an uncharitable word.

Therese was encircled by lovers—lovers of humanity and lovers of God.

As a grandmother I have many wishes for my grandchildren. But this one reigns above all else: I wish such an environment of love for them and for each and every child everywhere.

> *And now faith, hope, and love abide, these three; and the greatest of these is love.*
> **1 Corinthians 13:13**

October 2   Being Church

We, the people, are the Church! And from our years of parenting we have learned much about how to be the Church.

We-who-are-the-Church need to be constantly growing—lest we forget the past, lose touch with the present, and neglect preparing for the future.

We-who-are-the-Church need vigorous, life-giving roots like

those that nurtured the early Church. But we must never let the Church—ourselves—become root-bound. We are not to conform blindly to rules or to tradition but instead enthusiastically affirm our empowering heritage.

We-who-are-the-Church need to be open to the winged-guidance of the Holy Spirit, for it is only in freedom that we can effectively proclaim the ever-new message of the gospel.

We-who-are-the-Church need to remember that we are family—a diverse, lively, headstrong, compassionate, loving human family.

> *Proclaim the message; be persistent whether the time is favorable or unfavorable; convince, rebuke, and encourage, with the utmost patience in teaching.*

2 Timothy 4:2

October 3   Communication

The *words* of love, of God, of faith do not come easily to me; I speak them very hesitantly, even to my own children and grandchildren. The thoughts are there, but the words and the ability to utter them often are not.

I am even uncomfortable hearing others speak of such things. How flippantly some people spout these thoughts, making them sound hollow, almost sacrilegious.

But then I worry—do my children and grandchildren realize how much I love them?

Surely they all know, don't they?

> *And let us consider how to provoke one another to love and good deeds.*

Hebrews 10:24

October 4   Cakes

A baptismal day cake.

    A one-candled, jellybean-decorated cake.

    Heart-shaped Valentine's Day cakes.

Birthday cakes, topped with clowns or animals.

A First Communion cake.

Flag-topped 4th of July cakes.

A Confirmation cake.

Egg-shaped Easter cakes.

A graduation cake with diploma and mortarboard.

A "Welcome Home" cake.

A "Congratulations on Your Promotion" cake.

The multi-tiered, dream-filled, wedding cake.

Mother's Day—and Father's Day—cakes.

The cakes of increasingly precious anniversaries.

A shared-with-many retirement cake.

Profusely candled birthday cakes.

Wake and funeral cakes.

> *The LORD bless you from Zion.*
> *May you see the prosperity of Jerusalem*
> *all the days of your life.*
> *May you see your children's children.*
> *Peace be upon Israel!*

Psalm 128:5-6

October 5   Dogs

D ogs and kids are a lot alike. Both require time, attention, care, and love; both are expensive to raise, eat a lot, have a tendency to make messes, and need lots of training. Some experts gave me these guidelines for raising dogs:

You can't change the basic nature of a dog—so don't try. Concentrate on developing the good qualities of the dog you have.

Treat a dog kindly and the dog will respond accordingly. You can always recognize a dog that has been mistreated.

To be sure a dog is accepted by others, train the dog well. As one friend expressed it, "You don't do the dog any favors when you let the dog remain untrained or when you tolerate misbehavior."

Yes, raising dogs and raising kids have much in common.

Train children in the right way,
and when old, they will not stray.

Proverbs 22:6

October 6   Everywhere!

I see them everywhere. In stores and churches, parks and schools, places of amusement; on buses and trains and planes; in apartment building stairways and hotel lobbies—I see them everywhere. In suburban neighborhoods and barrios; in rural communities and inner-city tenements and downtown skyways—I see them everywhere.

I see sullen, disruptive, headstrong, uncooperative teens and young people. And with those rebellious youth I see worn, patient, struggling older people—parents and step-parents and guardians and grandparents and older siblings. For every instance of child abandonment or abuse or neglect—how many more cases are there of caregivers who do not give up on their responsibility. How many more continue to love and serve—despite moments of near despair.

O God of great kindness, reward abundantly the faithfulness of these bearers of your love—not only in eternity, but here on earth—and soon! Amen.

May the L<small>ORD</small> give strength to his people!
May the L<small>ORD</small> bless his people with peace!

Psalm 29:11

October 7   Confidence

A basic need of all parents is to feel secure within themselves and confident of their ability to parent.

There is a corresponding function we grandparents can perform for our offspring: supporting and encouraging them as the parents of our grandchildren.

How reassuring it can be to my children that I, knowing them as well as I do, communicate to them, in word and attitude and deed, "You can do it!"

In everything do to others as you would have them do to you; for this is the law and the prophets.

Matthew 7:12

October 8   Grandma Mary

I have difficulty relating to that slim-hipped teenage Mary pictured in Christmas stories, a young woman untouched by life, an unapproachable plaster/plastic female absorbed in prayer.

My favorite image of Mary is a composite of Mother Teresa, Dorothy Day, and Golda Meir. This Mary—a human, loving, wise, mature woman—has been tried by life and not found lacking. To me this woman is real!

I envision this older Mary with those gathered in prayer on that first Pentecost filled, for the *second* time, with the Holy Spirit. And just as she had previously devoted her life to the nurturing of her human-divine child, she surely must have then devoted her energies to the nurturing of the infant Church.

I envision Mary as the reteller of parables; as the inspiration of those first vital Christian women; as the keeper of family stories; as the advocate for the poor and oppressed; as the hospitable refuge of the first missionaries; as the wise adviser of the disciples; as the lover of Jews and Gentiles, slave and free alike; as the *bobbeh*, the Jewish grandma, laughing and playing with all the children.

Hail, Grandma Mary!

> *All these were constantly devoting themselves to prayer, together with certain women, including Mary the mother of Jesus.*

Acts 1:14

October 9   Always More!

Our language for God is restricted to metaphor, for we are attempting to describe the Infinite with finite vocabulary. Thus we desperately need a magnificent array of images to reflect the many and varied aspects of our God.

God-as-the-Creator is also imaged as the Cosmic Dancer, Eternal Holy Mystery, Weaver God, Transforming Laughter, Womb of Creation, Higher Power, Prime Mover, Our Mother, God of the Eternal Now, Divine Ancestor, *Yahweh, Elohim, El Shaddai, Adonai,* She Who Is, *Alpha* and *Omega,* Immanence and Transcendence, Eternal Goodness....

God-as-the-Christ is also imaged as the Cornerstone, the Word, Our Friend, Divine Healer, Teacher, Rabbi, the Good Shepherd, Lover, Our Foundation, *Emmanuel....*

God-as-the-Holy Spirit is also imaged as the Passionate One, Lady Wisdom, Source of Justice, the Hand of God, *Sophia*, Light or *Shekinah*, Eternal Fire, Breath or *Ruach*, Fire of Love, Indwelling Spirit....

But no matter how many and varied our images of God, God is always more!

> *"I am the Alpha and the Omega," says the Lord*
> *God, who is and who was and who is to come,*
> *the Almighty.*

Revelation 1:8

October 10   Human Beings

We are human *beings*.

But sometimes we lose sight of this obvious fact and think we are human *doings*.

We get caught up in the hectic pace of our complicated, fragmented society and confuse our priorities. We begin thinking that only those who *do* are important; we assume it is in *doing* that we find the meaning of life. By our lifestyle we give our assent to the culture's emphasis on personal achievements and possessions.

We have to remind ourselves that we are human *beings*; it is what we *are* that is important.

We are children of God and have been made in God's image. *That* is why we have value! Relationships and love and compassion—these are the important aspects of life; our lasting value is found in the good which our *being* brings forth in others.

We are human *beings*.

> *(Mary) sat at the Lord's feet and listened to*
> *what he was saying.*

Luke 10:39

October 11   Helping Others

What is the best way to keep busy?
Helping others.
What is an effective method to fight depression?
Helping others.
What allows us to keep balance in our life?
Helping others.
What is the unsurpassed antidote to loneliness?
Helping others.
What is the most efficient way to help ourselves?
Helping others.
Perhaps there's more sound psychology in the gospel message than we realize.

> *I was a stranger and you welcomed me. I was*
> *naked and you gave me clothing, I was sick and*
> *you took care of me, I was in prison and you*
> *visited me.*

Matthew 25:35-36

October 12   Investing

The banker, referring to his mother, said she "invested" in her family. "Some people," he continued, "say she spent herself on us, her family. I prefer to use the term *invested.* She invested *herself* in *us.*"

What a beautiful—and wise—analogy. We *invest* ourselves in our children and in our grandchildren. This investment profits us

and the young and the community and the world. Everyone bene-
fits.

> *For those who want to save their life will lose it,*
> *and those who lose their life for my sake, and*
> *for the sake for the gospel, will save it.*

Mark 8:35

October 13   Lay Spirituality

What is *lay* spirituality?" Recently, that question was
asked, phrased as though only the professed religious
or the ordained can be truly spiritual; as though we
laity are entitled only to the scraps from their holy and inspired
table. But might we have the matter turned upside down:

Christ was lay, for he was never ordained by any established religious group.

Christ preached mainly to lay people, using stories about farm-
ers, housewives, parents, children, and what we consider the lay
life.

Christ's first recorded miracle, requested by his mother, was at a
wedding.

When the apostles asked Jesus how to pray he addressed God
using a title associated with family life: Father.

In the Good Samaritan parable, the hero is not the priest or the
priest's assistant, but a lay person.

The Church claiming Christ's name is comprised overwhelmingly of lay people.

> *I am the way, the truth, the life.*

John 14:6

October 14   Manners

The mother's complaint was familiar: "I devote much of my life to my family—and that goes unrecognized. The younger kids take me for granted and the teenagers, in typical rebellious fashion, are critical of everything. They are all so unappreciative!"

"Did you tell them?"

"Yes—with predictable reactions: My husband understood perfectly and the kids completely disagreed. They believe it isn't necessary to be polite to family members. My legalistic teens maintained I'm just doing my duty and the younger kids said that since everyone knows we care for each other we don't have to bother saying it."

I nodded knowingly. "We show consideration to those we really don't love, and are inconsiderate of those we do love."

"Exactly! Many times I've sent the kids off to a friend's with a reminder about manners, concerned that they would forget to say 'please' and 'thank you' to others. What I should have done was remind the kids of their manners when they returned home!"

Let all that you do be done in love.

1 Corinthians 16:14

October 15   Orphans

For much of my life, whenever I heard the word "orphan" I thought of young children: the Little Orphan Annies of the world.

As I've gotten older, I've realized that there is another category of orphans: we who are of the oldest generation.

We "older orphans" must function without the practical guidance and wisdom of our elders. We must continue to grow, but without the presence of those who can nurture us from their experience. We are expected to offer leadership and insight to those younger than us, while we ourselves are often still in need. In our orphaned state we continue our life-adventure as abandoned explorers looking to the very heavens for guidance.

Might our *senior citizen facilities* be called *adult orphanages*?

> ***Father of orphans and protector of widows***
> ***is God in his holy habitation.***

Psalm 68:5

October 16   Planned Parenthood

There is an insidious fallacy lurking in the term *planned parenthood*, for it nourishes the delusion that parenthood, beginning with conception and continuing through all that follows, can be planned or controlled.

Conception is the beginning of life, and life abhors planning. Life is a mystery! A mystery to be lived, embraced, suffered through, enjoyed, plunged into, endured, absorbed, examined, learned from, delved into, experienced.

Rarely can it be planned.

> *Where were you when I laid the foundation of*
> *the earth? Tell me, if you have understanding.*
> *Who determined its measurements—surely you*
> *know! Or who stretched the line upon it? On*
> *what were its bases sunk, or who laid its corner-*

stone when the morning stars sang together and
all the heavenly beings shouted for joy?

Job 38:4-7

October 17 — Questions

Before the number of words in a youngster's vocabulary exceeds the number of the kid's fingers, the word "why" predominates. Kids begin early to ask questions; they ask to learn, to get attention, to please, to annoy....

Around adolescence, however, they have acquired the answers to all the important questions of life.

Only later do they begin to realize, with wide-eyed surprise, that they really do not know all the answers. Then the "why" questions are resumed.

Maturity is finally attained when they realize that life is lived within the mystery of questions unanswered.

Who do you say that I am?

Luke 9:20

October 18 — Only Child

The term *only child* has two different meanings. It can describe:

(1) A child fortunate enough to have no brothers or sisters;
(2) A child unfortunate enough to have no brothers or sisters.

There is speculation that the phrase *brotherly love* was first used by an only child.

> *For in Christ Jesus you are all children of God*
> *through faith.*

Galatians 3:26

October 19 Traditions

When I was new at mothering, I believed that only *religious* traditions had an impact upon the religious beliefs of children. While I certainly still believe in the tremendous importance of religious traditions, I now recognize the importance of *family* traditions. Ritual is an essential element to the welfare of the soul, and customs—religious or not—form the foundation for family unity and solidarity.

Traditions, if well-chosen, can unite a family, help nurture children, and offer stability to young adults. The family that has traditions—whether sacred, secular, hilarious, or reverent—is more likely to recognize the importance of liturgy and religious ritual.

If no foods evoke pleasant memories for us, then we approach the Lord's table at a disadvantage. We appreciate more fully the annual Christmas story if we are familiar with how Grandma and Grandpa courted and married. The events of Triduum are more meaningful to us when we know the pivotal events in our ancestors' lives. And if we never celebrate birthdays, how can Pentecost, the birthday of the Church, be filled with meaning? Hoorah for traditions—both old and new!

> *Posterity will serve him;*
>   *future generations will be told about the*
>   LORD,
> *and proclaim his deliverance to a people yet un-*
>   *born,*
>   *saying that he has done it.*

Psalm 22:30-31

October 20 We Who Mourn

It is *in* our mourning,
    in our grieving,
    in our pain and tears of loss,
that we find our consolation.
For our very mourning and grieving and weeping
testify to our love.

It is in and by God's love
that we are able to love.
And it is in and by God's love
that we are united with those we love.
Just as we cannot be separated from God's love,
so we cannot be separated from those we love.
Love remains,
for all love is of God.

> *For I am convinced that neither death, nor life,*
> *nor angels, nor rulers, nor things present, nor*
> *things to come, nor powers, nor height, nor*
> *depth, nor anything else in all creation, will be*
> *able to separate us from the love of God in*
> *Christ Jesus our Lord.*

Romans 8:38-39

October 21 Time

You'd really like her, Mom. She's great!" The boy was describing the grandmother of his friend. "She's almost as much my friend as Tom."

"Why is she so special?" his mother asked.

He paused to find the right words. "She always has time."

Time. Time tyrannizes everyone, especially parents. We know what it is like to be oppressed by demands and deadlines and people and crises. However, we have also learned that those things which clamor most loudly are rarely the most significant. Often the degree of noisiness is itself an indication of fleeting importance.

The tasks that have eternal implication are easy to postpone; the goals of lasting value may be ignored completely; the important activities in life often have no sense of urgency about them.

That young man gave a terse description of a woman who is, most probably, a very complex human being. Yet he described her to his own satisfaction in four words: "She always has time."

To kids T-I-M-E spells love.

> *I hope to come to you and talk with you face to*
> *face, so that our joy may be complete.*
>
> **2 John 12**

October 22 Self-Preservation

The instinct for self-preservation is certainly one of our strongest drives. We do what is needed to preserve our life, our bodily safety, our sanity.

When we grandmothers were bringing up our children, most of us were stay-at-home moms. That meant that we lived with our preschool kids twenty-four hours a day; that also meant that we lived with our school-age kids twenty-four hours a day during summer vacations, on holidays, and every weekend.

Certainly we made great effort to teach our kids manners and cooperation and consideration so that they might become productive members of society. However, we also demanded certain standards of behavior for our own sake. It was a matter of self-preservation—we lived with those kids!

Now many kids time-share their lives with Mom, with Dad, with step-parents, with baby-sitters, with daycare workers, with grandparents, with neighbors, with other relatives.

There is no one who has to live with them for twenty-four hours a day, seven days a week—and it shows!

> *As you have done, it shall be done to you;*
> *your deeds shall return on your own head.*
>
> **Obadiah 15**

October 23   Tears

Deep relationships abound with tears—tears of joy, sorrow, relief, frustration, happiness, fulfillment, rejection, entreatment, loneliness, hopelessness, accomplishment, pleading, gratitude, separation, reunion, hope.

Tears are signs of love.

> *Jesus began to weep. So the Jews said, "See how*
> *he loved him!"*
>
> **John 11:35-36**

October 24   United Nations Day

UNITED NATIONS DECLARATION OF THE RIGHTS OF THE CHILD.

"The right to affection, love, and understanding.

"The right to adequate nutrition and medical care.

"The right to free education.

"The right to full opportunity for play and recreation.

"The right to a name and nationality.

"The right to special care, if handicapped.

"The right to be among the first to receive relief in times of disaster.

"The right to be a useful member of society and to develop individual abilities.

"The right to be brought up in a spirit of peace and universal brotherhood.

"The right to enjoy these rights, regardless of race, color, sex, religion, national or social origin."

> *Jesus said, "Let the little children come to me,*
> *and do not stop them; for it is to such as these*
> *that the kingdom of heaven belongs."*
>
> **Matthew 19:14**

October 25   Alleluia!

Alleluia! I am celebrating!
    I celebrate this day because it is.
    I celebrate because I am.
In the presence of my many blessings, I celebrate.
In memory of past joys, I celebrate.
In anticipation of what is to come, I celebrate.
For what is now, here, today, I celebrate.
Alleluia! I am celebrating!

> *Praise him with trumpet sound;*
> *praise him with lute and harp!*
> *Praise him with tambourine and dance;*
> *praise him with strings and pipe!*
>
> **Psalm 150:3-4**

October 26   Socks

I love to tell the grandkids stories—selective ones—about their parents when they were young.

One grandkid's favorite story is of his father, Robert, and his uncle, Shawn, when they were teenagers.

Rob and Shawn had shared a common sock drawer for years. During this time, Shawn had conformed to the tradition of wearing matched socks while Rob, his older brother, had quietly rebelled against such convention. Considering it a waste of time to search for sock-pairs, Rob attained a certain notoriety for wearing mismatched socks. Actually, this was a practical way of utilizing all those odd socks that a large family somehow always accumulates.

And so, sharing the same sock supply proved to be a very suitable arrangement—until Rob left for college. The morning after the big departure, Shawn announced with indignation, "Rob took with him one sock from every pair!"

> *His mother treasured all these things in her heart.*
>
> **Luke 2:51**

October 27   Stories

Stories rank right after food, clothing, and shelter as necessities of life. We especially treasure Scripture stories, for they are the tales of our own family: great-great-great-great grandparents Abe and Sarah, cousins Daniel, Esther, Jeremiah, Isaiah, Elizabeth. Our Judeo/Christian family tree contains fascinating characters like Ezechiel and Peter, weight-lifter Sampson, musical Miriam, John the Hermit.

The stories we can tell about these fascinating people! They railed at God, balked at the tasks set before them, took up their duties reluctantly. They were angry, frustrated, tired, jealous, self-centered, discouraged. God has wisely presented them to us in all their humanity, including their failures, lack of virtue, doubt, sins, and, yes, their accomplishments and faithfulness. God's involvement with humanity is presented to us, not as philosophy or theology divorced from reality, but as the stories of real people steeped in day-to-day living.

Stories put flesh on moral truths, give life to theological principals, make history fascinating, inspire us to greater efforts, move us to action. The stories of Scripture are much like the stories a grandmother tells her grandchild.

> *We will tell to the coming generation*
> *the glorious deeds of the LORD, and his might,*
> *and the wonders that he has done.*

Psalm 78:4

October 28   "Stay With It, Grandma!"

How easy for my grandchildren to adapt to our high-tech world—they can't begin to imagine a world before TV or space exploration.

And so my life is invaded by computers and e-mail and the Web, cellular phones and voice-mail, CDs and video games and programmable VCRs, microwaves and fax machines and answering machines, and whatever else someone manages to imagine and then build.

"Stay with it, Grandma!" the kids say.

"I'm trying, I'm trying!" I answer.

> *Blessed be the LORD who has not left you this*
> *day without next-of-kin; and may his name be*
> *renewed in Israel!*

Ruth 4:14

Our first, most basic, relationship to God is that of creature to Creator. This profound fact of our existence extends beyond time and space; it existed before we humans became involved in discussions of doctrine, developed division in theology, and lost ourselves in the trappings of ritual.

This cosmic, primordial relationship between Creator and creature is most closely paralleled on earth in that special relationship between parent and child.

As we parent, we have an opportunity to gain insight into God's relationship to us as our Creator/Parent. As we learn of God's love for us, we grow in our understanding of and love for our own children and grandchildren.

Through parenthood we have been admitted into an empirical school of theology. We became lifelong students of these ever-changing, wonderful and painful, demanding and rewarding love relationships.

> *Our Father in heaven,*
> *hallowed be your name.*

Matthew 6:9

To have the trust
of a young person
is to shape the future.
The boy Samuel was ministering to the LORD
under Eli....Now Samuel did not yet know the
LORD, and the word of the LORD had not yet
been revealed to him....Eli perceived that the
LORD was calling the boy. Therefore Eli said to

Samuel, "Go, lie down; and if he calls you, you shall say, 'Speak, LORD, for your servant is listening.'"

1 Samuel 3:1,7,8-9

October 31 Halloween

I had agreed to help serve dinner at a homeless shelter on Halloween evening.

While I was busy with the cooking, serving, and cleanup, the shelter volunteers, who would be spending the night there, were also quite busy. They had brought pumpkins to be carved, apples for dunking, and other games to occupy the men and women who were the guests for the night.

Some of the homeless people participated in the activities; some observed from a distance; some ignored the festivities. For nearly all of them, the holiday was yet another poignant reminder of what had been, of what had never been, of what might yet be.

Being homeless is much more than being without shelter. Being homeless touches the core of who we are and who we hope to be.

Even the sparrow finds a home,
and the swallow a nest for herself,
where she may lay her young.

Psalm 84:3

November 1   All Saints' Day

The liturgy on the Feast of All Saints had progressed to the time for the sign of peace. The man in front of me turned around and enthusiastically grabbed my extended hand with both of his. "Happy Feast Day!" he said.

What a delightful way to be reminded that we are all called to be saints. We were all created with our sainthood in God's mind.

In wholehearted affirmation of God's plan and of who we are and who we are to be, we greet each other today with "Happy Feast Day!"

> *You are a chosen race, a royal priesthood, a holy nation, God's own people.*
>
> **1 Peter 2:9**

November 2   All Souls' Day

Today I remember women who have walked this earth before me.

Mothers: all those who nurtured me; *learned women* and *teachers*: Anne Sullivan, Mary McLeod Bethune, Margaret Mead, Elizabeth Seton; *healers*: Florence Nightingale, Elizabeth Kenny, Clara Barton, Elizabeth Blackwell, Virginia Apgar; *adventurers* and *risk-takers*: Harriet Tubman, Amelia Earhart, Joan of Arc, Christa McAuliffe; *religious leaders:* Hildegarde of Bingen, Mary Baker Eddy, Anne Hutchinson, Teresa of Avila, Julian of Norwich, Sojourner Truth, Catherine of Siena, Elizabeth Cady Stanton, Thea Bowman; *political leaders:* Golda Meir, Liliuokalani, Creek Mary, Louise Yim, Victoria, Josefa de Dominguez, Indira Gandhi; *musicians, dancers, artists:* Clara Schumann, Grandma Moses, Marian Anderson, Sarah Bernhardt, Margot Fonteyn, Helen Hayes, Coco Chanel, Mahalia Jackson, Georgia O'Keeffe;

scientists, engineers, mathematicians: Marie Curie, Rachel Carson, Maria Goeppert Mayer, Lise Meitner; *athletes:* Mildred "Babe" Didrickson, Suzanne Lenglen, Sonja Henie; *poets* and *storytellers:* Emily Dickenson, Murasaki Shikibu, Agatha Christie, Juana Ines de La Cruz, Elizabeth Barrett Browning, Mirabai, Pearl Buck.

I thank God for all the women who continue to inspire me.

> *Precious in the sight of the LORD*
> *is the death of his faithful ones.*

Psalm 116:15

November 3   Irene

I visited Irene in the nursing home recently.

Elderly, frail, kind Irene has already inspired the staff, just as throughout her active life she has left her characteristic mark upon all she encountered.

"How are you today, Irene?" I asked.

She smiled. "I can't do much these days, but that's okay."

"The nurses say you are a very easy-to-please patient."

"How can I have complaints? My needs are all provided and I am surrounded, filled with God's love. I just lay here and let God love me. And God does that very well!"

> *God is love, and those who abide in love abide*
> *in God, and God abides in them.*

1 John 4:16

November 4   Called to Faithfulness

We are called to be faithful because of other people;
We are called to be faithful in spite of other people
We are called to be faithful because of our successes;

We are called to be faithful in spite of our successes.
We are called to be faithful because of our weariness;
We are called to be faithful in spite of our weariness.
We are called to be faithful because of our failures;
We are called to be faithful in spite of our failures.
We are called to be faithful because of our lack of love;
We are called to be faithful in spite of our lack of love.

The one who calls you is faithful.

1 Thessalonians 5:24

November 5 · Domestic Abuse

The media is filled with accounts of domestic abuse—parents and children, husbands and wives, lovers. Our response is horror—at least until we become insensitive to its widespread prevalence. Yet surely, if there is one place that we should be safe, it is within the family.

Which makes me wonder, how would God use the term *domestic abuse*? For God is our Creator/Father/Mother; we are all one human family. Though we may use different languages and words to address our God, we are all God's children. Though we may have different lifestyles and religious practices and sexual orientations and cultural backgrounds and racial heritages, we are loved by our Creator.

And if we really mean that humanity is one family, then *all* the violence and brutality and injustice which we allow to exist in our world is *domestic* abuse.

As a mother weeps for her child who turns against brother and sister, so God, the parent of us all, weeps for us, and for what we do to one another.

Have we not all one father? Has not one God created us?

Malachi 2:10

Friends, neighbors, coworkers, family members all see us grandmothers differently. If pressed for what is significant about us, each one could probably come up with a terse descriptive statement:

"She has the cleanest desk in the office."

"She's a real golf-nut."

"Her garden is the most beautiful in the neighborhood."

"Her records are always up-to-date."

"She can identify birds by their calls."

"She tells the most interesting stories."

"She always sets a gracious table."

"She'll do anything for a friend."

How disquieting it is to realize that the multiple facets of our lives and the complexity of our personalities can be compressed into a description of so few words. Then again, perhaps others see the reality of us so much more clearly than we can.

> *I commend to you our sister Phoebe, a deacon of the church at Cenchreae, so that you may welcome her in the Lord as is fitting for the saints, and help her in whatever she may require from you, for she has been a benefactor of many and of myself as well.*

Romans 16:1

Unfortunately, example is the most effective method by which children learn.

Had God consulted *us* we would have voted for a

weekly lecture, a set of videos, or perhaps a how-to manual with a few easily absorbed principles humorously illustrated.

However, God did not ask our opinion. Perhaps the example method was chosen to improve three generations simultaneously.

> *Let your light shine before others, so that they may see your good works and give glory to your Father in heaven.*

> **Matthew 5:16**

November 8 Fixed Income

For all those years, we knew that when finances got tight, we did have some options. We could economize, watching expenses more carefully and reorganizing our list of financial priorities; we could work harder; we could put in more hours; we could do a little moonlighting; we might look for a different job; we might consider retraining; we could relocate. For all those years, we knew that through our efforts, we could improve the situation.

But once we enter the world of the *fixed income,* we realize our vulnerability! We are at the mercy of legislators and pension fund administrators and investment counselors and corporate take-over giants; we are helpless victims of the local and global economies with their roller coaster interest and inflation rates; we are eminently vincible.

Growing older requires several varieties of faith.

> *The LORD is my shepherd, I shall not want. He makes me lie down in green pastures;*

he leads me beside still waters;
he restores my soul.

Psalm 23:1-3

November 9 Water

The poet of Genesis speaks of the waters of chaos before creation. All living beings come from water; we ourselves are composed primarily of water; throughout our lifetime we experience a constant need for water.

Heaven-sent water, in the form of rain or snow, revives and restores our earth and us. Water is necessary, not only for our physical survival but also for our emotional well-being as we seek its splashing, flowing, babbling, cooling, restful, soothing, invigorating presence.

Sometimes child care appears to be a vocation preoccupied with the cleansing aspects of water, as when we are surrounded by dirty kids, dirty diapers, dirty clothes, dirty dishes, dirty walls, dirty floors—all awaiting our ruthless attack with water.

But water has other significant roles in our lives: the blessed water used at Baptism; the handfuls of water used to swab our feverish child; the cupful of water graciously given to the thirsty; the tears of joy, sorrow, remorse, forgiveness, shed for our young; the blessing water sprinkled over our remains at life's end.

All water is holy, for it is life's source and sustenance, and a sign of God's loving presence.

You visit the earth and water it,
you greatly enrich it;
the river of God is full of water;
you provide the people with grain,
for so you have prepared it.

Psalm 65:9

November 10   The Storm

The storm hit powerfully, unyielding to anything humanity had placed in its path. Our human smugness and security disappeared before this massive display of nature's force. Telephone and power lines were downed; transportation was halted. The most basic aspects of survival became extraordinary and unfamiliar challenges to our sophisticated ways.

In an instant, many of our modern conveniences were turned into useless burdens; our preoccupation with society's frills had made us incompetent for the tasks of survival.

Powerless before this unleashed force, we recognized anew our dependence upon those whose protecting and supporting services we accept without acknowledgment, on the unseen and under-rewarded technical workers who make possible our way of life, and on everyone who makes possible the complex functioning of our society.

To them we offer belated gratitude.

> *The God of glory thunders....*
> *The voice of the LORD flashes forth flames of fire.*
> *The voice of the LORD shakes the wilderness....*
> *The voice of the LORD causes the oaks to whirl....*
> *May the LORD give strength to his people!*
> *May the LORD bless his people with peace!*
> **Psalm 29:3,7-8,9,11**

November 11   The God-Quest

There are many different gods during the course of a person's life.

An infant is the god-center of its own existence—and

acts accordingly. However, the power and abilities of Mom and Dad gradually convince the child that it is they who are gods. Later a favorite teacher becomes a god of wisdom, who is quickly succeeded by other teachers, coaches, scout leaders, family members.

Then, at teen-age, the awesome peer-group-god comes into being.

The God-quest is a journey along these ever-enlarging concentric circles until, at long last, the searcher recognizes God as being beyond all these circles.

But what makes God God is that the Divine is able to love each one of us as though *we*, individually, are the center of *God's* universe.

> *Know that the* Lord *is God.*
> *It is he that made us, and we are his.*
>
> **Psalm 100:3**

November 12   Grandma's ABCs

Kids aren't the only ones with ABCs, for we grandmas have our own. Depending on the age of the grandchild, ABC means:

Always Bring Candy (Cookies, Chocolate);

or

Always Bring Coins (Cash, Credit-cards).

> *When the vessels were full, she said to her son,*
> *"Bring me another vessel." But he said to her,*
> *"There are no more." Then the oil stopped flowing.*
>
> **2 Kings 4:6**

The human need for stories is well-documented throughout the ages. And if we need stories, then we need heroes—both male and female—to people these stories.

Religions have heroes; societies develop heroes; cultures and subcultures nurture their heroes; families pass on stories of their own heroic relatives; races have their unique heroes; professions have their historic patrons; every group has people to emulate.

There are the larger-than-life characters in Scripture, the miracle-working saints; there are the buddhas and gurus and rabbis and mystics; there are the personae of the Greek, Roman, Scandinavian, Russian, Celtic, African, Indian, Polynesian, Latin American, Asian and Native American mythologies; there are the spectacular heroes of folktales and fables; there are the famous/infamous characters of TV and radio and movies and books.

We all have our own individual heroes. They are the people we try to emulate; their stories are the ones we relate to our families; they are the people we "canonize" in our groups and neighborhoods; their stories provide the dinner table topics. Who are my heroes?

> *From now on all generations will call me blessed.*

Luke 1:48

It takes some—but not very much—humility to admit we need God.

The real test of humility is if we can admit that we need

each other.

> *After (Jesus) had washed their feet, had put on his robe, and had returned to the table, he said to them, "Do you know what I have done to you? You call me Teacher and Lord—and you are right, for that is what I am. So if I, your Lord and Teacher, have washed your feet, you also ought to wash one another's feet."*
>
> John 13:12-14

November 15   Irregular Duties

Years ago we recognized the regular duties of parenthood: feeding, clothing, sheltering, teaching, loving these young of ours.

Somewhere along the way, however, we also encountered the *irregular* duties of parenthood, the tasks we could never have envisioned, such as chauffeuring the hockey team to the rink for a three a.m. practice; bailing out the rebellious youth with the DWI; learning more than we ever wanted to know about allergies or sibling rivalry or learning disabilities or gays and lesbians or hyperactivity or the intellectually gifted or....

Now that we have reached the *grand* state of parenthood, we are discovering that there are *irregular* duties of this vocation too. There seems to be no end to life's surprises.

> *Therefore I prayed, and understanding was given me; I called on God, and the spirit of wisdom came to me.*
>
> Wisdom 7:7

What words do I *write* today that will become a mantra legacy to my grandkids? Will they remember familiar words of wisdom? Or foolishness? Or impatience? Or acceptance and affirmation? Or condemnation? Or indifference? Or faith? Or compassion?

What words do I *say* today that will become a mantra legacy? Will they remember familiar words of wisdom? Or foolishness? Or impatience? Or acceptance and affirmation? Or condemnation? Or indifference? Or faith? Or compassion?

Or will the mantras be in the form of *touch* or *look*? Will they remember familiar responses of wisdom? Or foolishness? Or impatience? Or acceptance and affirmation? Or condemnation? Or indifference? Or faith? Or compassion?

Or will the mantras be my *deeds*? Will they remember familiar deeds of wisdom? Or foolishness? Or impatience? Or acceptance and affirmation? Or condemnation? Or indifference? Or faith? Or compassion?

What is my mantra-legacy to my grandkids?

> *I am reminded of your sincere faith, a faith that*
> *lived first in your grandmother Lois and your*
> *mother Eunice and now, I am sure, lives in you.*
>
> 2 Timothy 1:5

The word *myth* has at least two seemingly contradictory definitions. Myth may refer to something that is wholly fictitious, or it may refer to something that is more than simply true—it *is* truth or what is perceived as such.

This second type of myth is a poetic rather than a scientific answer to some of the questions which humanity has always asked. This myth conveys a point more completely than an actual happening cluttered with distracting details of dates and names. It overshadows the reality of the people involved or the event described; it justifies a belief or way of life. There are many such myths in Scripture which reflect, as to be expected, the society and beliefs of those times.

Myths survive, not because scholars in academia have kept them alive, but because ordinary people find value in the insights these myths offer us about life, relationships, the world, God. Because myths have tremendous power to influence our attitudes, convictions, actions, they always need to be assessed as to their effect.

> *So the* LORD *God caused a deep sleep to fall*
> *upon the man, and he slept; then he took one of*
> *his ribs and closed up its place with flesh. And*
> *the rib that the* LORD *God had taken from the*
> *man he made into a woman and brought her to*
> *the man.*

Genesis 2:21-22

November 18 Legacy

An inherited fortune, even an extremely large one, can be spent in a short time, as the Prodigal Son and many others have so well illustrated.

However, there is another kind of legacy that all of us, rich or poor, bequeath to our offspring and those around us. Our conferring of it carries through each hour of every day as we demonstrate our values and priorities reflected in our lifestyles.

This legacy consists of our standards of conduct, work habits, interactions with others, prejudices, heroes, points of view, fears, leisure activities, self-conceits, regard for the past, responsibility to the future, concepts of faith, ideals of beauty, and depths of love.

This legacy with which we endow our youth, in contrast to the inherited fortune, often lasts entire lifetimes.

Peter said, "I have no silver or gold, but what I have I give you."

Acts 3:6

November 19   Life

The Jews have a toast that says it succinctly: "*Lehayim*!" which translates "To Life!"

At this Thanksgiving season we celebrate and give thanks for our bountiful blessings. We recognize the harvest and our many blessings of the earth; we recognize family and relationships and love and heritage; we recognize achievement, wealth, education; we recognize our gifts of faith and community and tradition; we recognize our many freedoms. For all these we give thanks.

But none of these matters if first there is not life!

He asked you for life; you gave it to him—length of days forever and ever.

Psalm 21:4

November 20   Prayer

Whip those beads! Rattle off those prayers!

Sometimes when I pray, I am mouthing words that never touch my heart.

Sometimes when I pray, my mind remains unscathed by the passing phrases.

Sometimes when I pray, I do not realize what I am saying.

Perhaps I should think about the purpose of my prayer.

Do I consider prayer a *magical* activity?

Do I think I can *manipulate* God?

Perhaps I should think more about why I pray. For the bottom line of praying is to change *me*.

> **Create in me a clean heart, O God,**
> **and put a new and right spirit within me.**
>
> **Psalm 51:10**

November 21   Tough Holidays

The holiday season that is just beginning can be tough on families. For many of us caught up in the seasonal activities, there is never enough time or energy or money to do all we want to do. And who receives the brunt of our frustrations? Those closest to us—our families, our friends.

Today let us remember to love one another.

During the holidays we have more family get-togethers. Unfortunately, they do not always live up to the ideals as portrayed in the Norman Rockwell paintings or the TV ads or the greeting cards. Instead, we may have relatives who are sometimes cantankerous, or even impossible.

Today let us remember to love one another.

There are some among us whose hearts are aching with deep, deep pain, whose lives are torn apart by divorce, by family rifts that have become chasms, by death. Yet in the midst of the pain—and while in no way denying the pain—it is all the more important to focus on those who remain, and to be thankful.

Today let us remember to love one another.

> **In everything, O LORD, you have exalted and**
> **glorified your people, and you have not neglect-**
> **ed to help them at all times and in all places.**
>
> **Wisdom 19:22**

November 22   Together

The new, multi-purpose facility included both a senior center and a day care facility for infants and children. While economy of construction and centralization of services were major considerations in the planning, the proximity of the two centers is an added bonus to visitors.

We senior citizens, both those who are grandparents and those whose title is honorary, aren't afraid to establish close connections with children. And we aren't afraid to be childlike, reveling in spontaneity and frivolity, for we understand and respect childhood.

Fortunately, many seniors recognize that the special connectedness that can occur between a child and a grandparent-type can exist between people whose paths just happen to cross—even briefly at a neighborhood center.

> *Enter his gates with thanksgiving,*
> *and his courts with praise.*
> *Give thanks to him, bless his name.*
> *For the LORD is good;*
> *his steadfast love endures forever,*
> *and his faithfulness to all generations.*
>
> **Psalm 100:4-5**

November 23   The "Other" Grandma

How fortunate that my grandchildren do not have only one grandmother. How fortunate that they can be grandparented in more than one way.

But I have to remind myself that I am not in competition with the "other" grandma.

There are many ways to grandmother, and each of us brings her own unique gifts to the grandmothering role. We have different perspectives, different personalities, different lifestyles. But *different* does not mean that one way is to be judged better than another.

Like that munificent Dove of Pentecost, we bring a variety of offerings to our young—the most important being our individual selves. And no one else can offer that gift.

> ***By the grace of God I am what I am.***
>
> **1 Corinthians 15:10**

November 24   Toward the Light

Round and round they go, turned this way and that; here, there, moved back again.

But no matter how much or how often I turn or move those planters and pots and vases, the plants always turn toward the light. They may have to bend or twist or curl, but they always manage to face the light.

I think those plants have more sense than I have! How easily I can get confused about the direction of my life. I get distracted or tired or worried or anxious or depressed...and I don't look toward God's light.

Sometimes I even refuse to seek God's light.

But like my plants, if I want to stay healthy, if I want to grow properly, if I want to blossom, I need the Light of God.

> ***This is the message we have heard from him and proclaim to you, that God is light and in him there is no darkness at all.***
>
> **1 John 1:5**

November 25   Weariness

Weariness is a condition caused by large numbers, excessive quantity, endless repetition.

Weariness does not come with the first or second incident or question or problem or episode; weariness sets in with the thirty-fifth tool that has been lost and the 147th "No!" to the same juvenile-generated question; weariness occurs when confronted with the 286th running of the car pool, the 654th form to be completed, the 1,001st punching of the time clock, the 10,000th day of going to work.

Weariness not only fatigues our body; weariness can also drain the life of our soul.

There is only one way to combat this soul-scaring exhaustion, and that is to view these numbers and their causes from the perspective of The Infinite.

> *But you, take courage! Do not let your hands*
> *be weak, for your work shall be rewarded.*
>
> **2 Chronicles 15:7**

November 26   Rae-Ann

I have never forgotten Rae-Ann, a teacher of one of my kids. Rae-Ann was highly regarded for her teaching ability and her love of children. But her abilities extended beyond the classroom door, for she was also well-known for her skill in getting along with the parents of her students.

I remember asking her about this. "There's really no secret to it," she answered. "When I was in college I had a prof who told us that we, as teachers, should always assume that parents are doing what they believe is right for their child. My years of experience since then have convinced me that was wise advice. Even when I believe what they are doing is not benefiting their child—I assume that their motives are for the good."

Parents and teachers need to work together for the sake of the child. So do parents and grandparents.

> *Let us work for the good of all, and especially*
> *for those of the family of faith.*

Galatians 6:10

November 27   Roots

Children have an absolute right to roots.

Children need to know who they are, to know where they came from, to hear their family stories, to learn of their ethnic traditions, to participate in rituals of faith, to meet people who inspire them, to experience places and times that are sacred to their heritage.

Children need to feel accepted as they are, loved as they are. They need to feel established firmly within a supportive firmament of family, humanity, and God.

Children need roots, so that, nourished by these roots, they can exercise their wings.

> *The LORD is my rock, my fortress, and my deliverer,*
> *my God, my rock in whom I take refuge,*
> *my shield, and the horn of my salvation, my*
> *stronghold.*

Psalm 18:2

Wings are the means by which young people exercise their independence and uniqueness.

Their personal free response to the Will of God requires wings; their following the direction of the Holy Spirit requires wings.

The endurance and strength and vigor of those wings are dependent upon the depth and wholeness of their roots.

> *Very truly, I tell you, the one who believes in me will also do the works that I do and, in fact, will do greater works than these.*
>
> **John 14:12**

November 29   Sense of Humor

Whatever would we grandmothers do without a sense of humor? A sense of humor helps us:

smile in our discomfort;
grin at the 100th telling of a "Knock, knock" joke;
overlook kid-caused chaos;
appear appreciative when presented with unwanted gifts;
beam at our dirty offspring;
accept our own foibles;
hug our sticky grandkids;
adapt to aging;
accept death;
live life!

> *Make a joyful noise to the LORD, all the earth.*
>
> **Psalm 98:4**

November 30 "Soft and Squishy"

I love my Granny!
Granny never skips pages when she reads to me
and never tells me to hurry!

"And Granny's rich—
she always has money for ice cream cones
and wishing wells
and gumball machines.

"Granny likes to play games with me
and to look at old pictures
and tell stories from long, long ago.

"And—what I like best—
No matter where I hug her,
Granny's soft and squishy!"

> *As a mother comforts her child, so I will comfort you.*
>
> **Isaiah 66:13**

December 1 — Advent Symbol

Despite the assertions of the media,
Despite the claims of the advertisers,
Despite the declarations of the merchandisers,
Despite the objections of the prudish,
The symbol of Advent is a pregnant woman.

> *(The angel Gabriel) came to (Mary) and said,*
> *"Greetings, favored one! The Lord is with you."*
>
> **Luke 1:28**

December 2 — Sermons

We adults think of a sermon as a talk given by a priest or minister or preacher.

But young people regard any adult-given address directed at them and exceeding two sentences as a sermon.

No matter how eloquent, how carefully phrased or meticulously thought-out, a sermon is rarely as effective as example.

> *You shall love the LORD your God with all your*
> *heart, and with all your soul, and with all your*
> *might. Keep these words that I am commanding*
> *you today in your heart. Recite them to your*
> *children and talk about them when you are at*
> *home and when you are away, when you lie*
> *down and when you rise.*
>
> **Deuteronomy 6:5-7**

       Aging Gracefully

O God, let me age gracefully.

Though my future may include limitations,
let me never forget to be kind.

Though aging may bring undesired changes,
give me the fortitude and faith to be patient—
patient with those around me,
patient with myself.

Though times to come may bring emptiness,
fill me with your presence and your love.

Give me, Lord of All,
time to rid myself of excess baggage
and to rectify my mistakes.

And please,
let me retain a sense of humor—oh YES!

> *Hannah prayed and said, "My heart exults in
> the LORD; my strength is exalted in my God."*
>
> **1 Samuel 2:1**

       The Brevity of Life

I n recognition of life's brevity, I've begun an ever-growing list of
activities which squander my time, such as:
    engaging in family feuds;

using saucers with cups;
taking offense;
putting off learning;
ironing;
delaying kindnesses;
ignoring friends;
postponing fun;
neglecting rainbows;

. . .

. . .

. . .

(Wisdom) is a breath of the power of God.
Wisdom 7:25

December 5   Calm and Serene

I am calm and serene, for I reside in God's love.
My source of peace is within me, for my serenity is not dependent upon forces outside myself.
My source of peace is within me, for there dwells the Holy Spirit.

I am calm and serene, for I reside in God's love.
I relax, abiding in God's keeping.
When I relax, I empower those around me to relax also.
When I relax, I affirm God's peace within me.
I am calm and serene, for I reside in God's love.

> *Do not let your hearts be troubled, and do not let them be afraid.*
>
> **John 14:27**

237

December 6   Christmas Traditions

Traditions are important—both those hallowed by time and those which develop because of the changing lifestyle of a family.

The efforts that went into Christmases past have spawned the memories which are now part of Christmas present.

There are memories of church—the music, the liturgies, the environment decorated in noel beauty. There are memories of Christmas surprises and successes and visits and gifts.

And there is the shared humor of the Christmas failures: the year some of the presents were hidden so well no one could find them or the year the dog pulled down the Christmas tree.

With time, the retelling of travel difficulties and misfitting presents and labors-beyond-reason eventually add to the family lore and become part of the Christmas traditions.

These memories, told and retold, transform a group of people who happen to be related into a group of people who are family.

> *Remember the days of old, consider the years
> long past.*
>
> **Deuteronomy 32:7**

December 7   Christmas-Focused Grandmas

For us Christmas-focused grandmas there are only two seasons—Christmas and the rest of the year. Our annual reckoning begins and ends with Christmas.

For us, Christmas shopping is an all-year avocation. We accumulate Christmas gifts from visits to the kids, vacations, and senior citizen outings. We stitch Christmas stockings in Lent, paint holiday bells in May, and craft snow figures in August.

Being sentimental people, we are fascinated with holiday customs throughout the world. We are moved to tears by Handel's *Messiah*, revel in *The Nutcracker*, and are a soft touch for any charity that helps others celebrate Christmas.

The home of a Christmas-focused grandma is often cluttered with crafts-in-progress; the stove is covered with candle wax and the carpet is littered with yarn; the kitchen table is hidden under cards and address lists; the bedroom is unrecognizable because of gifts and wrapping papers.

However, we admit our single-focus proudly, for grandmas—like children—most readily understand and enjoy the wonderment and mystery and love that is Christmas.

> **Glory to God in the highest heaven, and on earth peace among those whom he favors!**
>
> **Luke 2:14**

December 8 Everywoman

In our nation's capital is the National Shrine of the Immaculate Conception, for it is under this title that the United States is dedicated to Mary.

The heritage of many peoples in the United States include devotion to Mary under varied titles: Our Lady of Lourdes; Our Lady of Perpetual Help; Our Lady of Knock; Our Lady of Czestochowa; Our Lady of Fatima; Our Lady of Mount Carmel; Our Lady of the Pillar; Our Lady of the Miraculous Medal; and Our Lady of Guadaloupe—the feast day celebrated December 12th.

We have a multitude of images of Mary: a woman with the slanted eyes of an Asian; a dark-complected woman dressed in Mexican attire; a black woman in African tribal garb; a woman in Eskimo attire; a woman in Native American dress; a Middle-East woman in traditional garb; a sari-clad woman sitting in the lotus position; a woman looking like us.

Mary is for every woman.

And Mary said, "My soul magnifies the Lord,
and my spirit rejoices in God my Savior....for the
Mighty One has done great things for me, and
holy is his name."

December 9   "Don't 'Honey' Me!"

Don't call me 'Dearie' or 'Sweetie'!
    "Don't assume that just because I'm older I'm incompetent!

"Don't think that because I've lived many years my today is less important than yours!

"Don't presume that because I wear multi-focal glasses I lack insight!

"Don't conclude that grey hair means I'm hard-of-hearing!

"Don't assume that weakness of muscles means weakness of will!

"Don't patronize me!

"And don't 'Honey' me!"
    I have called you by name, you are mine.

December 10   G-R-A-N-D-M-O-T-H-E-R

Grand, generous, gifted, good-natured, gracious, genial, gleeful, graced, genuine, good, godly, graceful, guiding;
    Remarkable, resolute, receptive, reassuring, romantic, reconciling, refreshing, rejoicing, relaxed, real;

Admirable, adept, accomplished, amiable, amusing, affirming, affectionate, approachable, authentic;

Nice, notable, noble, needed, necessary, neighborly, neat, narrating, noteworthy, natural, novel, nurturing;

Dandy, daring, dignified, distinguished, deserving, diligent, delightful, discerning, devoted, doting;

Marvelous, magnificent, merry, moral, mirthful, multi-talented, mellow, merciful, magical, made-to-order;

Outstanding, openhanded, original, observant, optimistic, openhearted, offering, older-but-better;

Terrific, tremendous, trustworthy, talented, tenacious, tender, trusting, true, tailor-made, tradition-keeping;

Helping, honorable, happy, hospitable, holy, hallowed, heart-warming, high-grade, humorous, honest, helpful;

Encouraging, enjoying, exalted, excellent, eminent, esteemed, ethical, empowering, exemplary, endowed;

Regal, reverent, restful, respectable, reliant, remembering, renewing, responsive, reliable, resourceful, revered.

I will bless you, and make your name great, so
that you will be a blessing.

Genesis 12:2

December 11 God's Prayer

Maybe *God* should pray to *us*!
We find it so easy to rattle off prayers to God, asking God to do everything.

We pray for world peace—but follow our words with inaction.

We pray for good health—but fail to live in a healthful manner.

We ask God to change other people—but don't consider changing ourselves.

We pray for the poor—but do nothing to alleviate the injustices causing poverty.

We pray for the reconciliation of divisions—but refuse to trust others.

We pray for the environment—but do not change our lifestyle.

We pray for an end to violence—but continue in our preoccupation with violence.

We pray for a less materialist society—but continue to indulge our consumerism.

Maybe God, weary of our hollow prayers, has a few choice intercessions for us!

O *that today you would listen to his voice!*

Psalm 95:7

December 12 "Highs"

We all need "highs"—those experiences of total involvement resulting in an acute consciousness of our own existence.

"Highs" are found in *creativity*: painting, designing, decorating, inventing, wordsmithing, composing; in *quiet*: meditating, sunset-watching, praying, beach-combing; in *learning*: studying, solving, probing, analyzing, reviewing, questioning, researching; in *daring*: skydiving, racing, mountain-climbing, scuba-diving, ski jumping; in *accomplishing*: building, repairing, sewing, restoring, refinishing; in *competing*: participating in games, playing in tournaments, racing against the clock, setting new records; in *sex*: experiencing the oneness that comes from love and loving and being loved; in *involvement*: choral singing, political campaigning, protesting, acting; in *helping*: teaching, leading, directing, advising, listening, encouraging; in *activity*: dancing, skiing, gardening, biking, golfing, birding, reading, fishing, skating; in *working toward a goal*: attending college, writing a book, raising a family, building a boat, learning a trade.

We all need "highs." The most effective antidrug "program" is an environment in which other "highs" are demonstrated, welcomed, modeled, encouraged, nurtured.

In him was life, and the life was the light of all people.

John 1:4

December 13 "It Is God's Will!"

How very carefully we need to monitor our use of those powerful words: It is God's will.

Where do we say them? Standing alongside the newly dug grave? Waiting in the critical care unit of the hospital? Viewing the scene of a traffic accident or a natural disaster?

If those are the only times we assign responsibility to God, what does that tell our young about God?

Where is God's will on the joyous, fulfilling, deeply satisfying occasions? The much prayed-for healing, the long-sought reunion, the realization of dreams—are not these also God's will? Why "God's will" at the death of a nineteen-year-old...and not at the active, vigorous, productive life of the ninety-year-old?

Love and justice on earth is God's will for us in time; happiness in heaven is God's will for us in eternity.

I came that they may have life, and have it abundantly.

John 10:10

December 14 Mentors

We all have a need for mentors.

We need people we respect and want to emulate; we need people from whom we can learn; we need people whose compliments we seek and cherish.

We also have a need to be mentors.

We need to know that others respect us and want to emulate us; we need people we can teach; we need people we can compliment and encourage.

Grandmothering is a splendid, ready-made opportunity to be a mentor. How wonderful to mentor someone we love.

> *You did not choose me but I chose you. And I appointed you to go and bear fruit, fruit that will last, so that the Father will give you whatever you ask him in my name. I am giving you these commands so that you may love one another.*

John 15:16-17

December 15   Letting Go

Letting go is not passivity. Letting go is not giving way to weakness. When we *consciously* and *willingly* let go we are engaged in a variety of positive activities:

We are expressing our belief in the ultimate good of God's will;

We are admitting our own limited humanity;

We are recognizing others as unique creatures of God;

We are expressing faith in those other persons;

We are moving into a constructive way of thinking;

We are turning to God—a powerhouse of possibility;

We are expressing our belief in the Holy Spirit—who directs not only us but others too.

Those who think that *letting go* is a sign of weakness have never tried it.

> *Come to me, all you that are weary and are carrying heavy burdens, and I will give you rest. Take my yoke upon you, and learn from me; for I am gentle and humble in heart, and you will*

find rest for your soul. For my yoke is easy, and
my burden is light.

Matthew 11:28-30

December 16 Quest

The efficiency experts advise us to write down our specific goals—like owning or building a new home, getting a college degree or financially helping our kids/grandkids through college, opening our own business, writing a book, taking a world tour, owning a cabin on a lake/in the mountains/by the ocean.

But these specific goals reflect an overriding purpose as we venture forth on our own quest for the Holy Grail. Is that purpose financial security? Popularity? Power? Independence? Recognition?

Or is our quest for acceptance? A feeling of belonging? Holiness? Unity with family? Unity with humanity? Unity with God?

It is the quest that is said to purify our hearts; it is the purpose that is more revealing than the goal; it is the journey itself that transforms us even more than the arrival at the destination.

What is my life's quest? And what does that say about me?

For where your treasure is, there your heart will
be also.

Matthew 6:21

December 17 Meditation on Meditations

Why don't you write a meditation on writing meditations?" my husband asked.

"Now there's a novel idea," I responded, immediately wondering what in the process might be of interest to others.

Of course, I could describe my constant battle with panic lest I become paralyzed by the thought of having to write nearly 400 reflections!

As I write I find myself being more open to life around me—how else would I ever produce all these different thoughts? And so I watch, feel, live life more fully because of this task. I evaluate and wonder and pray more consciously; I listen all the more closely to the words of wisdom from others; and I try, very hard, to remain open to the whisperings of the Holy Spirit.

Perhaps the message is that everyone should write a meditation on her job, profession, hobby, or role as wife or parent/grandparent. The meditation could address ways to avoid panic or boredom or exhaustion or discouragement or overcommitment. It might include mention of the skills developed, insights gained, lessons learned. And, finally, there is the absorbing challenge of choosing an appropriate Scripture text.

We are God's servants, working together.
1 Corinthians 3:9

December 18   Mere Platitudes

Some people seem to speak mainly in platitudes; they mutter bumper-sticker sayings in response to every occurrence in life.

And I, wondering if they have any comprehension of the complexity of the situation, tend to dismiss their simplistic responses as lacking integrity's depth.

Yet I know others who, after much learning and scar-producing searching, after an overwhelmingly convoluted personal quest, discover a key that unlocks the meaning of life for them.

These seekers then realize that the hard-earned concept can be summarized rather briefly: "God loves us"; or "All we can do is do our best"; or "Let go and let God"; or "We are made in the image of God"; or....

How can these be dismissed as *mere* platitudes?

Our God comes and does not keep silence.

Psalm 50:3

December 19   Solemnity

The Scripture scholars claim that most of us miss the humor in Scripture. This thought takes us by surprise—is there humor in Scripture? Surely something as important as Scripture should be filled with and received with solemnity.

But we non-scholars of scripture approach the sacred texts at a disadvantage. We are only casually familiar with the culture and customs of those ancient times; we are not able to read Scripture in the original languages, so we miss puns and word-plays; and, perhaps most importantly, we approach Scripture with solemnity, not exuberance.

We humans often take life too seriously. We often take ourselves too seriously. And perhaps, we even take God too seriously.

As some great soul has asked, if laughter and humor and joy are gone—does God remain?

David danced before the LORD with all his might.

2 Samuel 6:14

December 20   Shopping

Struggling to complete my shopping, I was irritated and full of self-pity. My arms ached from carrying the awkward bundles, my legs ached from all the walking and standing in line, and my thoughts overflowed with resentment over how I had ended up with the lengthy shopping list.

While rushing around a corner in the mall I abruptly stopped. Before me were two wheelchairs proceeding slowly through the mall. The man in the second wheelchair was laboriously pushing the wheelchair ahead of him.

I stood there, ashamed of my mental complaining, for as they turned to enter a store I saw that the man in the first wheelchair had neither legs nor arms.

> *You are the God of the lowly, helper of the oppressed, upholder of the weak, protector of the forsaken, savior of those without hope.*
>
> **Judith 9:11**

December 21   Storytellers

Grandma, tell me a story!" *In the beginning, ever so long ago, people told stories. They told stories around campfires; during journeys without end; in the dark to drive away the inner darkness.*

"Nonna, tell me a story!" *The stories were about great deeds of men and women; about spirits; about gods and goddesses; about how the earth was created, how people came to be and why we are as we are; about times past and how the present came to be, and what is to come.*

"Grossmama, tell me a story!" *Stories were told and sung from generation to generation. "Again!" the children cried. "Another!" the people insisted.*

"La Abuela, tell me a story!" *To be the tribe's storyteller was to be honored; to be the village's wisdom keeper was a privilege, for the past was a treasure, and the stories were the people's wealth.*

"Babka, tell me a story!" *That was how it was in the beginning and how it is now. Much has changed; nothing has changed.*

> **Sing to the LORD, all the earth. Tell of his salvation from day to day. Declare his glory among the nations, his marvelous works among all the peoples.**
>
> 1 Chronicles 16:23-24

December 22   Stuff

We spend the first half of our lives acquiring *stuff*.

If we are fortunate, there is one brief moment in time when need and desire and possessions are all in balance.

Following that ecstatic moment, we come to the realization that every extra thing we own is extra trouble. We then launch into the second half of our lives, trying to rid ourselves of *stuff*: unnecessary items, paraphernalia, junk, forgettable mementos, gadgets, objects, articles, never-used possessions, knick-knacks, unwanted belongings, sundries that are "too-old" or "too-new," "too-small" or "too-big"....

It's all *stuff*.

> *Therefore I tell you, do not worry about your life, what you will eat or what you will drink, or about your body, what you will wear. Is not life more than food, and the body more than clothing?*
>
> Matthew 6:25

December 23   Teaching and Learning

When I anticipated parenthood, I envisioned that I, as the parent, would be teacher to my children. I did not realize how much I would learn from the experience of parenting.

Of course I had expected to acquire some needed information—like becoming familiar with the stages of child development and theories of learning and sacramental preparation procedures and rules of sports and 1001 ways to get kids to raise money for a worthwhile cause. I also learned how to organize a car pool in three and a half minutes, the proper hospital emergency room procedures, and basic parental survival techniques.

But much more importantly, through parenting, I learned—and continue to learn—about myself, about other people, about love and love relationships, and about God.

There is so much that God is trying to teach us about the Divine through our parenthood—and this continues into grandparenthood. What a wonderful, priceless, unbelievably enlightening opportunity for insight into the love which God, our Parent, has for us.

> *See what love the Father has given us, that we should be called children of God; and that is what we are.*
>
> **1 John 3:1**

December 24   The Why

Why do we do it?

Why all the shopping and gift-buying, the baking and cooking, the card-sending and letter-writing, the partying and decorating and visiting?

Why? Because of people, of course! People are the focus of all this effort—just as people were the reason for the first Christmas. People are what make Christmas, for without those we love, the tinsel and lights and carols are without meaning.

Christmas is about people and family—not just those related to us by blood or marriage, but all of humanity.

The power of love carries us beyond traditions or decorations, freeing us to celebrate even when we are in pain, enabling us to reach out from our solitude to touch others in their solitude.

The power of Christmas is the love that has lasted two thousand years and it is that love which we celebrate with our singing and gifting and decorating.

Christmas epitomizes the love of Christianity.

Everything has become new!
2 Corinthians 5:17

December 25   My Humanity

Today, on this feast of the Incarnation, I celebrate *my* humanity!

I affirm my birth-marked and age-spotted and often weary humanity. My marvelous and divinely imaged humanity.

I affirm my much-blessed humanity. The gift of life has come from the womb of God; humanity and our very earth have been blessed by the presence of the Incarnate One; and we—I!—have been chosen by the Holy Spirit as a dwelling place.

I affirm my embodiment. I celebrate my senses and my sexuality; my passions and my desire for intimacy; my physical abilities and awareness.

In thanksgiving for the Incarnation, I affirm my sacred and sacramental humanity.

All this took place to fulfill what had been spo-
ken by the Lord through the prophet: "Look, the
virgin shall conceive and bear a son, and they
shall name him Emmanuel," which means,
"God is with us."

Matthew 1:22-23

December 26   What Is Hope?

When success and achievement elude us and yet we do
not despair, it is because of hope.

When doubts and questions consume us and yet we
remain resolute, it is because of hope.

When our own limitations besiege us and yet we risk once again,
it is because of hope.

When the daily battles are never won, only endured, and yet we
find the strength to rise anew each day, it is because of hope.

When faith, commitment, forgiveness remain our constant com-
panions, it is because of hope.

> *May the God of hope fill you with all joy and*
> *peace in believing, so that you may abound in*
> *hope by the power of the Holy Spirit.*

Romans 15:13

December 27   Four-Letter Words

Now that the family's gone, I've composed a new list of
four-letter words that are not allowed in this house, such
as *cook, iron, dust*....

While the word *pack* could be on the list since it represents a job
I detest, it is allowed to be spoken since that task is necessary for

vacations and travel—and I'm all for going places!

Of course, there are other four-letter words that continue to be much honored here: *play, pray, read, rest, help, love....*

> **Seek good and not evil, that you may live.**
>
> **Amos 5:14**

December 28   Someday, Perhaps

Someday, perhaps, I shall be among the very elderly.

Someday, perhaps, I shall be unable to do the things which now occupy much of my time.

Someday, perhaps, I shall be unable to see or to rise from my bed.

Someday, perhaps, I shall have to be content with memories.

This day I must tuck away into the recesses of my mind to preserve for that someday: today's joy; today's people; today's consolation; today's loveliness; today's mercy; today's grace.

I will live today fully, so that my memory shall always retain the beauty of today.

> **O God, from my youth you have taught me,**
>   **and I still proclaim your wondrous deeds.**
> **So even to old age and gray hairs,**
>   **O God, do not forsake me.**
>
> **Psalm 71:17-18**

December 29   Being Let Go

We parents and grandparents are besieged with reminders that we have to *let go* of our young people. But who ever reminds those same young that they also are to *let go* of us?

The young have these frozen-in-time pictures of us that they carry with them while they grow, mature, travel through life. We are not allowed to change; we are not authorized to venture further on our life's pilgrimage; and we are most certainly not permitted to lose all those abilities we had in our prime.

Ah, but that is not life. And none of us—kid, grandkid, parent, grandparent—is to be held rigid by the bonds of either memory or wishful daydream, no matter how loving those bonds.

> *Now the LORD is the Spirit, and where the Spirit of the LORD is, there is freedom.*
>
> 2 Corinthians 3:17

December 30   Firsts and Lasts

s another year draws to a close and we begin thinking of the one to come, how easy for us to recall other *firsts* and *lasts*.

As parents we noted our own children's *firsts*. But witnessing at close range the development of our kids makes us even more appreciative of those grandkid-miracles of firsts—first steps, first spring, first words, first birthday.

We continue to celebrate even more grandchildren *firsts*: riding a bike, learning to count, turning a cartwheel; reading a book, writing a poem, being in a play; graduating and working and marrying and parenting.

All these *firsts* lessen our anxieties about our own expanding list of *lasts*—which is one more benefit of grandparenting.

And so, the last days of this favorite year are rapidly yielding way to the first days of a new favorite year, filled with happiness and sorrows, doubts and questions. In faith and with joy I now affirm: This year, soon to begin, is my favorite year!

Thus says the LORD...I am the first and I am the last.

Isaiah 44:6

December 31   The Year

Deep within is a spirit of eternal spring, buddingly alive, young and curious.

Deep within is a summer woman, brimming with compassion and understanding, energetic and strong and laughing.

Deep within is an autumn wisdom, mellow and intent, singing.

Growing within is a winter's shadow, stretching toward eternity.

Life's year is in me and I in it.

My heart chooses its own season.

For everything there is a sea on, and a time for every matter under heaven.

Ecclesiastes 3:1

Other Books of Interest to Parents

Daily Meditations (with Scripture) for Busy Parents
Tom McGrath
The perfect book for parents of both flavors. 256 pages, $9.95

Daily Meditations (with Scripture) for Busy Moms
10th Anniversary Edition
Patricia Robertson
The classic bestseller revised for today's moms. 256 pages, $9.95

Daily Meditations (with Scripture) for Busy Dads
Patrick T. Reardon
For dads of every age with kids of any age. 368 pages, $9.95

Our Common Life
Reflections on Being a Spouse
Mary and Rob Glover
Over 100 reflections for married couples. 120 pages, $5.95

Christmas Presence
Twelve Gifts That Were More Than They Seemed
Gregory F. Augustine Pierce, ed.
Twelve wonderful stories about the deeper meaning of holiday gift giving. 160 pages, hardcover, $17.95

**Available from booksellers or call 800-397-2282
in the U.S. or Canada**